728 Lenox Avenue

Haliburton Home Squared

To: Mr. & Mrs. Hooks

Thank you for your support.
Save
Our
Daughters
And
Sons!
You are an inspiration.

Francene Haliburton-Francis, Ed.D.

Love,
Francene

ISBN 978-1-64258-770-8 (paperback)
ISBN 978-1-64258-780-7 (hardcover)
ISBN 978-1-64258-771-5 (digital)

Christian Faith Publishing, Inc.
832 Park Avenue
Meadville, PA 16335
www.christianfaithpublishing.com

Printed in the United States of America

Contents

Preface

This is a book of poetry. It expresses the impact personal childhood memories have had on my adult life. It also reflects the influence those memories have had on how I managed encounters and conflicts with other people in my career in education. The person I am and the educator I've grown to be have both been shaped by my family, my African American culture, my Christian faith, my experiences with managing conflicts, and my experience with race relations.

A delicate balance and a terribly thin line exists between using compassionate, tolerant, and merciful responses to correcting children's inappropriate behaviors and using fair, firm and nontolerant judgment. Both approaches should demonstrate that discipline is an important ingredient of love. My siblings and I were blessed to have been reared and disciplined by parents who measured for that balance and walked that line. I am weighed down with stories I believe worth telling about the influence my childhood memories have had on my life. This book removes some of that weight.

I share several narratives, but the reader should not mistake this book's intended genre. This is a book of poems, my life in lyrics. The narratives were added to bring awareness to those readers whose memories and experiences have been different from my own. People like me exist and add value to an understanding of the American culture. We must be given a chance to grow and to evolve without being prejudged for our mistakes nor for the color of our skin.

For those who have similar stories of childhood memories and experiences as mine, I hope my poetry is able to tap into your stories and speak to your heart. Barack Obama explained in his book, *Dreams from My Father* that the tradition in Nairobi is to refer to your childhood home as Home Squared, "home twice over" (Obama

2004). I processed an understanding of myself and my life's experiences in the safety and comfort of 728 Lenox in Waco, Texas, Haliburton Home Squared.

Waco, Texas

What are you always
Bad-mouthing Waco for?
Waco is the door
Into and out of Central Texas.
Waco lets us dive into the action
North, south, east, or west of us
In a two- or three-hour drive.

Austin's action draws you south.
Continue the route, and San Antonians
Will tell you all about
What it cost to become a Texan.
In less than two hours north
Waco can deliver all sorts of fun.

Dallas has something to offer everyone
Young, old, modest, or bold enough not
To care what others think about
What they've got going on.

If Houston's scene is the one for you
Drive due east of Waco's calm and peace.
Houston hosts and houses
Most of everything that exists
Anywhere in the whole world, but
Is that where you want to rear your boys and girls?

Waco makes the best home.
Here the weary can return from their tours
North, south, east or west of Waco and
Feel safe and rest peacefully
Until their next adventure away.

The Wonderful World in Waco

Waco is where I learned to live.
It gives me pride and pleasure
To measure my childhood memories
Against those of friends
Who migrated in
From Dallas, Atlanta, Detroit, and LA.

When I weigh what Waco offered me
I see no difference in value in
The things that matter.
Watching the Brazos River's flow
Was enough for me to get to know
The power of water in motion.

It took my eight-year-old cousin
When I was eight, so I can relate to
The memories of my Memphis friends'
Fears of the Mighty Mississippi.

The Alico Building scrapped Waco's sky and often
I used it like a compass
To find my way home.
After being gone on an out of town trip
My family was met by Waco's welcome mat.
The Alico's bright red letters would lift
Our spirits like Lady Liberty's torch.

The Alico Building

Jesus lived and attended church in Waco
As well as in New York and Chicago.
Citizens made Central's memories in Cameron Park.
We had two YMCAs.
They used one and
We used the one built for us.

I attended Waco's schools and
Learned to read, to write and
To obey rules that keep
Our society great throughout
These United States.

We picked up candy
Dropped by the Shriners at the
Heart of Texas Fair and Rodeo Parades and
Waved at all the beautiful white women on the
Green and Gold Baylor Homecoming floats.
Come compare your notes with mine.
I'm sure you'll find that
Waco provided a wonderful world
In which boys and girls like me learned to live and
To deal with those
Who hated that we were here.
Waco yet provided and still provides
A wonderful world in which to live.

The Bledsoe-Miller Recreation Center

Bledsoe-Miller was once only a park
Where my family celebrated the
Fourth of July all day and
When it got dark
The fireworks would fill the sky
With temporary wheels of colors.
The building and other things were added
In later years.
Here Wacoans created memories.
We can recall
Decades of fun-filled laughter
Within the same walls that
We cried tears from the disasters
We faced there as well.
Placed near the river where Doris Miller and
Jules Bledsoe had a chance to know and
Love some of the same sites in Waco
Which can be seen today.
The bridge suspended between two worlds
Marked where the world of wealth ended and
The beginning of a world of poverty
A world yet loved
For the novelty of experiences offered within it.
Join me for a walk down Elm Street and
We can repeat the walks Miller made getting
From home to school.

Jules Bledsoe sang first for the saints at
New Hope Baptist Church on Fourth Street.
You can meet people there today and
Ask about the way of life Bledsoe
Left behind for a world stage.
Bledsoe and Miller made Waco proud and
Crowds of people, today, enter and enjoy
The Center that bears their names.

The Suspension Bridge

Walk across Waco's Suspension Bridge and
Rid your thoughts of the tensions threatening your peace.
Relax and release your cares with each step.
For more than a century
The Bridge has kept the secrets spoken
By those with broken hearts as well as those with
Hearts opened wide to love.
Suspended high above the river's flow
You can go see sites from the other side.
Waco's beauty cannot hide from you here.
Look north, south, east, and west.
Waco offers something for every guest
Who comes to spend time with us here
From faraway places or places that are near.
Come unwind your mind in our peaceful dimension.
Refresh yourself at Waco's Suspension Bridge.

The Brazos River Monster

The ghastly, green monster
Moves with a fast and fearsome flow.
The ripples threaten to pull below
Anyone who even dares venture too close.
Should one enter by choice or chance
The circumstance will have the same results.
The victim's gulps are no match for
The monster's relentless waves of rage.
The Brazos wages war against
All creatures who breathe air to live.
The River does not forgive
Those who trespass.
The Brazos River will dash to death
Hopes and dreams.

The Brazos River Shore

No need to jump nor rush away.
Sit safely near my peaceful shore.
Spend more time here, yielded and still.
I will tell you what you are missing
If you will only listen and
Wait for me to speak.
My advice can keep you calm
While you think your way
Beyond the storm that
Drove you to my side.
Confide in your river.
I will deliver your words
When my journey ends
To a friend
Who will carry them
Even further from you.
Like the water in your river,
This too shall pass.
Sit still and I will give you peace.

I was born in Waco, Texas, in 1959. I was the fifth child out of six children born to an optimistic black man, William and his wife, Delois. Although they were disappointed that the new branch on their family tree was to be occupied by a fourth girl, they named me, took me home, and loved me.

The person I am and strive to be evolved from reflecting upon significant events in my life and their impact upon my physical, intellectual, emotional, and spiritual development. Childhood experiences are crucial because they create memories that shape character.

I was an unusual child in that I had an uncommon ability to understand the consequences of contention as well as the rewards of amity. Unfortunately, this understanding was not in sync with my naivety as a child to believe that Utopia was attainable if you worked at it. As a result, I felt a personal obligation and responsibility to "right the wrongs" I perceived. Most, about which, I was unable to do anything.

This self-imposed obligation to bring joy and peace where there was contention led me to perfecting a fearless, independently-happy facade. While I busied myself with the emotional concerns of others, my own emotional concerns went untended, unbeknown to me, as well as to others who loved me. As I entered my adolescent years, this façade seemed to anesthetize the sensitivity and understanding I needed from those whom I had successfully duped into believing that I was happily self-reliant.

When I mistakenly inferred that they did not care, my actions became selfish and self-indulgent. Consequently, the negative influences of peer pressure during my teenage years became more valuable to me than the training I had received in my home and the achievements my parents had dreamt for the little girl they took home from the hospital. I lost sight of the difference having a good education could make in one's quest for happiness. As a result, my grades in junior high school took a plunge from the high averages I had been accustomed to receiving in my earlier years of education.

I received the first years of my education at Dripping Springs Elementary, a segregated African American school in my neighborhood. During these years, three significant events occurred that forever changed the course of my life and my educational experience.

The first event was the marginal defeat of an optimistic, young, black candidate for county commissioner of Precinct 3. That candidate was my father. I had had an opportunity to accompany him throughout the county as he pursued the campaign trail. Historical changes were taking place in America, and those changes made my father, and others who supported him, optimistic about the changes of which they could become a part. Although I was too young to realize the significance his being elected would have meant, I knew that it was important from the effort I observed him putting into the campaign.

That defeat not only affected my father greatly, but it also affected me. The death of his optimistic vision blocked my view of an optimistic future. I had shared with him in the pursuit of the campaign trail. I had shared with him in the victory of the first election that resulted in a run-off election. When defeat came to him after the run-off, it was my self-imposed obligation to help him recover and get back onto the highway to Utopia. I was eight years old.

The second event that was to change the course of my life occurred in the same year. My five siblings and I joined the statistics of children being reared in a single-parent home. My parents divorced. At a time when I felt that my father needed me most, the courts ordered that my mother should have custody of us, girls. (For the next six years, poverty shadowed the lives of my sisters and me, and the lessons we learned about frugal living are yet engraved in our memories.)

The custody of my only brother was awarded to my father. I can still recall the emotional stress of feeling helpless against the course of events. I felt an obligation and responsibility to change what was happening, but I could not.

The third life-changing event occurred two years later when my school district decided to integrate their schools. The era in which this transition took place did not dictate that the administrators should execute this task with wisdom and diplomacy. As a result, threats of violence, rebellion, and insurrection festered. We, children, were innocent victims of factions who struggled against a new system of education, which was here to stay.

After other eventful encounters with the growth of an integrated educational system, I eventually graduated from Richfield High School in 1977. My vision in regard to having a degree was still impaired, and my plans for the future did not include college, but rather marriage.

My mother, thank goodness, fought adamantly against this and exercised her executive power to coerce me into one semester at the local community college, McLennan Community College. Although my vision had not gained total recovery, experiencing sixteen weeks of college life did succeed in eradicating my marital plans. After overcoming other obstacles, in May 1983, I addressed my classmates during our commencement ceremony from Paul Quinn College and charged them to conquer the challenges that life will hurl at them at us. I had grossly overestimated the distance our country, sweet land of liberty, had traveled to overcome racial inequality because of the differences I saw between my parents' generation and my own generation's experience with race relations.

Daddy and me in the driveway with the family pet, Tippy

Mama in 1961

Mommy

Mamas die. My earliest memories of my mother caused me to generalize the life expectancy of mothers. After all, it was Mama who told me that she had a mother, but her mother was dead. She also told me that my father had a mother too, but his mother was dead. In fact, the mothers of all adults close to my loved ones were dead. I was too young to connect the other fact that those mothers were dead too because my mother's mother was also the mother of my mother's siblings and the same was true of the reason the mother of my dad's siblings were dead. My grandmothers were dead, and the grandmothers of all my cousins were dead. Mamas die.

In addition to the false conclusion I had about mothers dying based on confusing facts, my earliest memories of my mother were of seeing her in bed sick for days at a time. It was such a relief to see that she was still alive day after day whenever I was able to sneak a peek at her through my parents' opened bedroom door.

Because she was ill and in a house full of young children, Mom's door stayed closed, so she could rest. I would position myself, so I could see her whenever Daddy, Judy, or Bruce would go in to feed her, to give her something to drink, or to give her medicine.

Mama had asthma. She would have severe attacks that would render her bedridden for what seemed to me to be days and days. Like most men I knew in the 1960s and even a few women, my dad smoked. Smoking and asthma produce a deadly combination. Second-hand smoke threatened my mother's life every day, throughout the day.

In her thirties, my mother's body frame was slender. She was 5'8 and probably weighed 160 pounds. (I am guessing from memory.) At 5'8, she seemed to tower over me. She was gentle and tender-hearted, but she could be tough. She was not one to be messed with. I knew when she meant business. I obeyed her, not out of fear, but out of love.

Mama was a naturally beautiful young woman. She rarely wore makeup. She had a head of thick, black hair. It was not particularly long, but it was healthy with potential to be lengthy. It complimented her flawless caramel, smooth skin. She had a bump on the tip of her nose. (She eventually had it removed.) As was the fashion of the day, she had one shiny gold front incisor.

Mama had a slender neck. She referred to it as long and skinny, but I did not see it that way. Her arms were healthy and strong. She had a scar near her right wrist. When I would rub her arms, I would pause and rub the scar repeatedly. The skin on the scar was a slightly darker complexion than the skin surrounding it. It was more than an inch long and nearly half an inch in width. I must have asked her a hundred times about how she got that scar, and she repeated that story every time I requested it.

I never grew tired of my mother's stories. Her patient character always made me feel comfortable about asking her to tell specific stories again and again. Her stories always had a happy ending. I would ask her the same question after hearing the end of the story about how she got that scar. I would ask as I rubbed it, "Does it hurt?" She would always give me the same answer, "No." It was the happy ending that I had come to expect and that I needed to hear.

When Bruce was about four years old, his favorite television hero was a masked man called Zorro. Zorro wore a cape. His weapon of choice was a sword. Mom would use a safety pin to secure a bath towel around Bruce's neck to serve as a cape. Bruce would run around the house swinging half of a curtain rod, imitating Zorro's wielding his sword. One time, Bruce was playing Zorro while Mama was ironing. He swung his makeshift sword and knocked the iron over onto Mama's wrist. She was burned badly. It hurt when it happened, but as happy endings go, it no longer hurts.

My mother's hands seemed to always be in motion. I would watch them and admire them. Sometimes I would hold them in my hands, stroke them, and inspect their beauty. They were so much larger than mine. They were strong. She kept them clean. She lotioned them with Jergens, so they were soft. The length of her nails distinguished their white tips. She wore her high school class ring on her left ring finger.

Mom had long, beautiful legs. I can still see how sophisticated she looked when she would put on a pair of stockings and slip her feet into a pair of black pumps. Although she would try to avoid wearing stockings with runs, her legs even looked good in them. I remember praying and asking God to let me be as beautiful as my mother.

Mama was so much fun. She would tell fairy tales as well as family tales. She made us aware of and proud of our heritage as Vonners and as Haliburtons. She taught me phone numbers and how to use the phone. She taught me how to draw stick people and houses. She would say, "I can't draw, but I will draw one for you." She taught me "to try."

Mama would sing and teach us, Cheryl and me, songs. Mama could not sing, but she would try. We were able to learn the words to nursery rhymes and other songs from her, but she could not teach us to carry a tune because she could not carry one. In later years, much later years, she learned to sing, but (if you can imagine it), her voice of our childhood was worse than Edith Bunker's voice from the seventies hit series, *All in the Family*. Mom taught us by example to make an effort. She taught us to try.

Cheryl and I spent a great deal of time with our young mother. Mom would get Judy, Bruce, Rita, and Nita off to school. The television and I kept Cheryl entertained. *Captain Kangaroo* came on at 8:00 AM, Monday through Friday. I can't remember the programming order, but I do remember the programs we watched following *Captain Kangaroo*. We watched *The Beverly Hillbillies, Andy Griffith*, and *I Love Lucy*.

Sometimes Mom would babysit for her friend's grandchildren. Bernard and Gretel were cousins, born about the same time to two of Mrs. Phenix's daughters. It was easy to mistake them as twins because they were delivered and picked up by the same person. However, they did not look alike. Bernard was a brown-skinned boy, and Gretel was a light-complexioned girl. (African Americans refer to her complexion as "yellow," meant as a complimentary descriptor.) Both babies were beautiful. They were my first experience with caring for babies. I watched Mom and assisted her with fetching supplies and other tasks that saved her steps.

My version of my mother's life unfolds in two volumes. Volume I is where stories about her during her years as a wife would be found. Volume II would contain the stories about her as a divorcee. Although she was the same woman, the challenges she faced in each volume were so different that stories about her may make her appear to be two different women. Becoming the head of household suddenly of a single-parent home of five daughters required her to go from assistant home manager to sole manager. Mom was a natural at handling business. She proved to be fit for the task.

In 1969, during the time that her divorce became final, Mom was driving a blue and white 1951 Chevrolet. There were times that it would start quickly, times it would eventually start and times it would not start at all. It left a trail of smoke everywhere we went. It would putt along, making sounds as if it were choking on its own smoke. It managed to transport us to and away from home. My sisters and I were embarrassed to be seen riding in it. My mother was just proud to be managing her finances, proud to be independent and proud to be owner of a car. (We had friends living in two-parent households with either one car shared between both parents or no car at all.)

Mom drove that car until she upgraded in 1971. The upgrade was a 1959 Ford. Its description was exactly as its predecessor's description: blue and white, smoky and putt-putting along. It was no less embarrassing. It could possibly have been more embarrassing to us because we were older and cared more about the perspectives of others. Mom could not have cared less about what others thought of her car. It got her and her family where we needed to go and got us home safely. She was managing her home and finances. She was independent, and she owned her own car.

Those "jalopies," as we called them, took Mom everywhere she needed to go whenever they were running. Mom went to PTA meetings and neighborhood association meetings. She took us to band concerts and competitions for school. She dropped us off at movies, parties, friends' homes, and all of our other engagements in those cars. Mom even provided transportation for our friends who needed a ride to and from wherever we needed to go.

Once a month, on Sunday nights for years, whatever jalopy was providing transportation would take us to pay utility bills after church. The electric company, the telephone company and the gas company were on the same street, a block away from each other. The water company was on the next street, yet only a block away as well. It was somewhere to go and something to do as a family that cost us nothing.

We were too poor to spend much on entertaining activities, so we provided our own entertainment within the activities that we either had to do or activities that were free. Cheryl and I were in Girl Scouts. Judy was in Upward Bound until she graduated high school. Rita and Nita were in Upward Bound from ninth through twelfth grades. Mom's old cars took us and sometimes our friends wherever we needed to go.

Mom went to work Monday through Friday. She always kept a full-time job with benefits after she divorced. She went to church on Sundays for morning and evening services. She went to mission on Tuesdays. She took us to and from Youth Meeting on Wednesdays and choir rehearsals on Saturdays. Some Saturdays she was forced to go to the Laundromat to wash. She went grocery shopping on Friday evenings. This was her life for years and years.

Other places Mom would go accordingly for years were to visit Grandpa in Elm Mott (seven miles away from Waco) to visit the homes of her three siblings a few blocks away from our home on Lenox in different directions and to visit Aunt Helen, my dad's sister, across town. Besides our elderly next door neighbor, Mrs. Coffey, Mom had two additional close friends whom she would visit: Mrs. Tabitha Jefferson and Mrs. Jimmie Payton.

Jimmie was easily identified as Mom's best friend. They rode to work together. They talked on the phone daily. They gossiped together. They supported each other. Most importantly, they laughed together. Whenever Jimmie was around, we all laughed. Jimmie was a three-hundred-pound, natural-born comedian. (My mother needed to laugh in the beginning years of her divorce.) Jimmie kept her laughing with every visit until her death in 2002. Jimmie and my Aunt Olivia (Vonner) taught us that you did not have to be famous or on television to be as funny as famous people or comedians on television.

In 1969, Mom was an attractive divorcee with six children, five of whom she had custody, and they were girls. We learned years later that a wise, old lady in our church had cautioned my mother about getting another husband. Her words were, "Don't bring no man into your house with all them girls."

I can remember my mother only going on one date in the months following her divorce. Years later, she started a nine-year relationship that never resulted in marriage. Mom never remarried. The closest she ever came to being in love and feeling appreciated was in a relationship she had with a widower, the father of one of our childhood friends and our neighbor. They were in their middle ages.

Mom did not drink beer, wine, or alcohol. She did not go to clubs. She did not dress provocatively. She did not entertain "boy-friends," in our home like today's young mothers and grandmothers. I cannot begin to imagine how some children feel when they hear their mothers engaging in sexual activities with men they have brought home. Some children even adjust to seeing the faces of different men emerging from their mothers' beds and exiting their homes. Some of these young mothers today don't even bother trying to hide their drug and sexual activities from their children.

My mother's name and moral character warranted respect. She has lived her life caring and providing for her family. She has considered no sacrifice for us too great. She has earned her daughters' best service and care in her twilight years. She will reap the spoils of her labor because she showed us how to care for her by her example in caring for us. Young mothers and grandmothers don't have to be as conservative in their appearance and social activities as my mother was, but I encourage them to consider how they live among their children/grandchildren. They should want to be someone their children and grandchildren and the friends of their children and grandchildren can respect for the right reasons.

Like millions of mothers and daughters before have and those after us will have, my mother and I both survived the generation gap between us. Rearing me through my teenage years was no picnic for her. She was a conservative, godly woman trying to mother a fun-loving, smart-aleck, rebellious daughter. I was so different from my mother's other conservative daughters. We were all taught right from wrong. Although I was not as obedient to my mother as they, I did not disrespect her. Not that much. I say "not that much" because I believe that disobedience is disrespectful, and I could be disobedient.

Parenting is not easy. Parents have to have a variety of tools in their toolkits. The tool that works this time may not work next time. The tool that works to correct this child may not be effective with correcting another child. My mother had to use tools to correct me that she never had to use on my siblings. My behavior was far from extreme by today's standards, but back then, to be labeled a "good girl," you had to do and say what was expected. I would question Mom, "Why?" or "why not?" I never became disrespectful toward Mom when she corrected me. I was raised to be respectful, and I yet value it as a social skill and survival skill.

I caution young students I have to discipline as an assistant principal about their social skills. They expect to exonerate themselves from the consequences of disrespectful behavior. They try to convince me that they could not help themselves. They had to cuss at a teacher. They had to tell a faculty member what they were thinking. They had to say what was on their mind even though they knew it was wrong, and they would be in trouble.

I try to get those young people to think about how they are setting themselves up for failure in the work force. Many of them make improvements. They know my advice is good because they have personal stories of their own or stories from close relatives and friends who have failed in the work force due to disrespectful behavior.

When we fail to abandon the habit of saying what we think without considering the consequences, we may not control ourselves at a crucial moment. After all, it is a habit. In the workforce, disrespectful behavior will get you fired. Most young people have thought about that point. What they have not considered as a consequence for disrespectful behavior in the work force is that it can also keep you from being promoted on a job, and it can keep you from getting a good reference and recommendation to be employed at a different company. Being respectful is an essential social skill. Parents who do not teach their children to be respectful are doing their children a disservice.

After coming home from work, my mother would relax to a cup of coffee and a copy of the local newspaper. We knew not to bother her or the newspaper before her "coffee and newspaper treatment." Mother enjoyed milk and sugar in her coffee. She preferred a brand of canned milk called *Pet.*

Sometimes, before my teenaged years, I would serve Mom her coffee. She would instruct me in how much sugar and how much milk to add to her brew. I am not certain about remembering how much sugar she wanted, but I will never forget how I measured the amount of milk to add. Mom would say, "Make my coffee the color of me." Mom was a caramel color in those days. I would add milk into Mom's coffee until the color was smooth, beautiful, and inviting because that is the way I saw Mommy.

Mama was so wise. She planned her work then worked her plan. She attacked every problem with a step-by-step strategic plan, especially problems that required money to solve. She sacrificed and from time to time forced us to also make sacrifices until she had enough money to execute her plan.

Mom had pride and taught us to have pride too. We qualified for free lunch at school, but we never ate free lunches. Grandpa had money, but we never asked him for help financially with one exception. (Mom paid him back every dime. He was pleasantly surprised and proud of her success to keep her word.) Aunt Dot and Uncle Ted, Mom's sister and her sister's husband, also had money, but Mom did not borrow money from them for quick solutions to her financial problems.

When the toilet needed to be replaced, we flushed it manually with a bucket of water. We kept a bucket in the restroom for the exclusive purpose of flushing the toilet. We would fill the bucket with water from the bathtub faucet as often as necessary to flush our waste thoroughly. We used this procedure for longer than a week or two. Eventually, Mom was able to purchase a toilet and pay a plumber to replace the broken one.

Then there was the time that the hot water heater busted. We had no hot water in our home for more than a couple of weeks. While waiting for Mom to scrape and save enough money to replace the broken one, we developed an appreciation for a functioning hot water heater. We had to boil water for every task that required hot water.

What is the least amount of water you can bathe in comfortably? We once could answer that question based on how many pots of water one was willing to boil and add to a tub of cold water in order to take a warm bath. Those were also days that demanded cooperation among us. De facto rules developed out of common courtesy such as the following:

- Leave your water for someone else to use if it is clear enough for reuse.
- Don't bathe for so long that clear water that someone else could use would no longer be warm enough to be comfortable for the next person.
- Don't use water someone else has boiled without their permission.
- Say "Next" once you've emptied your hot water from the pots, so the next person can start boiling her water.
- Boil the water to rinse the dishes while you wash the dishes.
- Use a large container to make the water a comfortable temperature before you pour it on your head to shampoo and rinse your hair.

For longer than a week or two, the kitchen sink had a leak. Until Mom was ready to work her plan to fix it, we monitored a bucket strategically placed under the sink. When the bucket accumulated water, we emptied it into the yard out the back door. That area cultivated the most beautiful green, healthy grass in our entire yard.

Mom planned the meals for the six of us every day for years. She shopped for the ingredients, paid for them, and directed traffic for where items were to be stored according to the order she planned to cook them. She cooked every day once she was home from work and had read her newspaper. She learned to do so much with stretching a pound of ground beef and varying the ways chicken could be prepared. We never went hungry, and we always enjoyed the meals Mama prepared.

It was always a treat when Mom made dessert. I can still see her standing over a stove stirring a liquid in a boiler until it thickened. It was not meant to be eaten hot, so we had to wait for the dessert to chill in the refrigerator. We were so excited to hear her tell us that the banana pudding was finally ready. She baked peach cobblers and tea cakes and other cookies and cakes. When she baked cakes, we would "call" for the utensils from which we wanted to lick the batter. Someone would call, "I got the spoon." Someone else would call one beater. Still another would say, "I got the other beater." Usually two people got to "lick" the mixing bowl. This process required one to use her finger to encircle her share of the bowl repeatedly until no more batter could be retrieved. Our home was full of examples of cooperative spirits.

We had Baptist Training Union books in addition to Sunday school books. We would remind each other on Saturday night to study the Sunday school lesson while Mom was finishing her Saturday chores. The Training Union books, however, came with a daily Bible reading. If you did not read your DBR scripture every day by midnight, you could not receive credit when you completed your BTU envelope on Sunday evenings. It was in the spirit of cooperation that the Haliburton girls helped each other get our points. One would find the scripture in the Bible, read it, then pass the Bible to the next sister until we had all read our daily Bible reading.

Those were great days to be growing up. It was important to our parents for us to have a Christian education. We maintained the discipline under my mother's supervision even after our parents divorced.

On Saturday nights after everyone had finished her daily Bible reading and studied her Sunday school lesson, we would sit around the television dressed for bed and watch the 10:30 PM programming and eat ice cream. What we actually ate was called mellorine, a less expensive tasty ice cream substitute. Mom purchased it in a rectangular box.

We would consume the entire box in one sitting. Nita would raise the lid and use a table knife to mark lines that measured the block of ice cream into six even pieces. Cheryl and I would watch Nita carefully to be certain everyone received her equal share. If the marks did not appear even, Cheryl and I would force Nita to erase her marks and make another effort to divide the block evenly. Whenever Mom did not want her share, an announcement was made to determine who wanted an equal measure of Mom's share.

African American women owe a debt of gratitude to Madam C. J. Walker. She developed hair care products and methods for African American hair in the 1890s. Her methods included the use of heated combs (biography.com, retrieved 7/18/2017). Our hair has extremely different texture than the hair of white people, and must, therefore, be managed differently. African Americans learned and yet struggle with learning to love and appreciate the difference even if whites reject our self-appreciation.

In 2007, a morning talk show host, Don Imus comfortably called the African American women of the Rutgers University's basketball team, "nappy-headed hos" (Ryan Chischiere mediamatters. org, retrieved 7/18/2017). Nappy-headed is a derogatory term all too familiar in the African American community in reference to our hair. We collectively spend millions of dollars in our efforts to distance our appearance from this descriptor.

Mama had very little funds to contribute to the millions accrued toward caring for African American hair, yet she had five African American heads-of-hair for which to care, and her own coiffure made six. Mom used Madam C. J. Walker's tried and true methods of heated combs to care for our hair. We call it straightening or pressing hair. Mom used a burner on the kitchen stove to heat the comb that straightened our hair.

We would wash our hair, comb it out, let it dry, section it off, and wait our turn to have our hair pressed on Saturdays. As we got older, we had to alternate which week we got our hair pressed. It became too much work for Mom to try to do five heads in one day among her other Saturday chores. What memories!

The time spent with Mom while she pressed your hair was also your private time with her. She talked with you about the things she wanted to discuss with you, and we talked to her about the things we wanted to discuss with her, especially things we did not want the others to know. The time spent getting your hair pressed was time spent bonding with Mama.

Mama would navigate us through the process amidst our conversations. We knew what she meant and what to do when she would say,

- Hold still.
- Catch your ear.
- Turn your head this way.
- Hold your head down.
- Move your finger.
- This part is not dry.
- You did not comb this section out good.
- Hold your head back.
- Don't flinch.
- I'm almost through.
- I just have one more plait.
- I'm going to have to get this a little closer.
- Go tell Nita (or whoever was next) to come on.
- Now go brush it and roll it.

Thank God Mama had learned how to care for our hair. She could not afford to pay someone else to do it. We could not afford the embarrassment of not having it done. We attended school with girls who did not keep their hair because they could neither afford a hairdresser nor did they have someone who could keep their hair for free. Girls whose hair was unkempt were, sadly, treated differently at school, at church and in our communities. Mama spared us that despite our state of poverty. Thank you, Mom. Thank you, Madam C. J. Walker.

Mama in 2013

Thank You, Mom

I found so much power in your smile
When I was a child growing up to be
The person I am today.
There was never anything or anyone
To fear as long as I could hear that
Your voice meant you were nearby
If I felt a need to call out.
The power in your touch was full of so much love.
The sight of you gave me joy.
Your love had the power
To make whatever was wrong, right or
So it seemed.
My life's survival leaned and depended
Upon your ability to make a way
Day after day,
Years out and years in and even
When the years pressed beyond a score
With no more than a,
"Thank you," in return
From a grateful heart.
You taught my heart
To appreciate and to demonstrate
An attitude of gratitude
For all gifts, great and small.
You know more than
All creatures under God's sun
The value of the words, "Thank you, Mom."

The Color of Me

"Fix my coffee the color of me," Mom would say,
But Pet Milk in a can could never
Make coffee look the way
Mom's color looked to me then or even today.
I could taste her coffee for Imperial's sweet success
But Pet could not pass Mom's Beauty Contest,
"The Color of Me."
Pet could not duplicate Mom's glow.
Pet did not know that Mom's color emitted
Signals of tender, loving care.
Mom's silky, soft, smooth cinnamon color
Could not be matched by any other source.
For God Himself had endorsed Mom's color
At her birth
But pleasing her, made my efforts
Worth every try.
My mom drank every cup as though it were,
"Just right."
Never knowing my fear that it might not be
As requested,
"The Color of Mommie."

Teach Me

Teach me to use the phone, so
Once everybody's gone
I can call Granddaddy
To find out when he will come.
Teach me to tie my shoes, so
I can get used to seeing that
Learning is a process and
Repeating the lesson over and
Over again, patiently is
What great teachers do and
Mom,
No teacher was better than you.

Teach me why I must go to church and
Search for God's will for my life.
Teach me to strive to do what is right.
Teach me by your gentle, loving light
To know and always look for the glow from
The Light of the World and
I will always be
Your "sweet little girl," and
Forever His.

Delois

Evil staked his claim and
Mispronounced her name, saying
"The Lowest,"
Hoping to create
The coldest, poorest, soarless
Life of lovelessness,
But Jesus shared the secret joy
Coded in His own name.
He spelled it with a smile and
Gave her the power
To spread His love, comfort, and cheer
Even while
Turmoil threatens peace.
He has the name above every name and
The power to give value to any name.
Jesus released her from the curse and
Delois is valued above rubies.

Deeds of Love

Whether the child support was in the mailbox or not
We all had to eat, and
Have shoes to protect our feet, and
Have air from summer's heat and
Coats to keep us warm from winter's cold.
Mom, you managed every
Load you had to bear, and
Seemed to have something left
To share with others
Who needed your love and your care.
You met our needs and so much more.
Your deeds of love will live forevermore.

The News

When it came to the news
Mama could choose her source.
Jimmie never missed a beat and
It was a real treat to get from her
The rest of the story.

Mrs. Jefferson sometimes brought the news
While other times
She was the news and
She even used to take news away and
Report what others had to say.

From time to time Aunt Olivia would stop and
Drop some news we had not heard
Because like Jimmie,
Little birds were always bringing her news that
Channels 6 and 10 couldn't begin to report.

But Mom could depend on her sources
To know the news from places
She did not choose to go.

Mama's Home

Mama's home from work.
Perk her some coffee.
Give her the newspaper and
A minute to rest from the
Labor she just left at the job.
Briefly mob her
For a minute of her time and
Then leave her to unwind her way.

Let her pray and leave the cares
In her heart at the altar of God.
When she can feel refreshed
A family meal
Will be prepared and
Shared with all who come to eat.
At night, she'll sleep
While God keeps all her little ones safe.
The evil thoughts of the day
Have all been chased away.
All enemies of love have gone
All because Mama's home.

YooHoo

Rather than using a phone
"YooHoo was our neighbor's
Call to Mom for,
"Are you home?"
When she would call across the fence
Out the door my mom soon went.
Mom would go next door to visit and vent
As young women often do
With sage, wise women who
Have already conquered
Life's greatest threats and
Are willing to share their joys and regrets
With anyone who lets them
Sit on the lawn and chat.
Mrs. Coffee was just like that.
Years turned her hair
From silver to white and
Changed her height from its stately, upright position
To a shorter one with a slight
Hunch in her back.
You, who raised your girls alone,
Protected them and provided them a steady home
You, who went to work
Twelve months a year
Year after year,
Hear my words again and again

When times get tough.
You have enough within you
To make it through
Any storm that comes your way.
Just keep going every day.
You will get there.
YooHoo!
You will get there.
Her mind remained as sharp as a tack
Even after the laughter between her and Mama
Was weakened by Mrs. Coffee's failing health.
We recall the wealth of wisdom in
The YooHoo call to Mom.
You, who have been my friend
Even as my life comes to its end.

Sunday Night Ride

Once a month, on Sunday nights
The phone, water, gas, and lights
At home were on Mom's mind.
She'd find the time
Right, after church
To deliver the bills
She had worked so hard
Planning a way to pay.
She'd drop them off
One by one and
Would not stop
Until all were done.
When the bills were paid
We felt her pride.
She had assured us all during
The Sunday night ride.

First

When my life's experiences have been at their worst
Mama was always the first
Person I turned to for help.
She kept me from
Being ridiculed to scorn.
She fueled my discouraging moments
With powerful encouraging ones.

When trouble, sickness, needs, and lack
Pinned my hopeless, helpless
Back against the wall
So convinced that I would fall
The very first person
I could always, always call
Was my loyal, loving Mama.

Mellorine

We ate mellorine from a box
Rather than ice cream
That costs lots more.
It was Mom's Saturday night treat.
Even when there was nothing else sweet to eat
There was always mellorine.
Poor people everywhere
All have a story they can share
About a special treat
That reminds them of
Their mother's tender, loving care.
For my siblings and me
It was mellorine ice cream.

Wake Me

Wake me and
I'll wake them.
I'll make their lunches for school.
I'll pull them out of bed if I must.
I'll do what's necessary, so
They won't miss the bus.
I'll hold the bus, so
They won't get left.
I'll take care of them and myself.
Go to work, Mom.
We will all be fine.
Don't spend time worrying about us.
Trust God and you will see.
He will meet our needs.
Just wake me.

The Car

We have a car, but
We are ashamed to be seen in it.
Even when it's clean,
It's still old.
We've been told by our peers
To the point of tears that
Our car is a joke.
It bellows smoke.
It putt, putt, putts along and
Others poke fun at us
As we drive by.
Why do we have to be so poor?
The doors squeak.
The wheels repeat their creepy sounds
As they go round and round
Shaking us around inside
Making it impossible for us
To ride and sneak past those
Who point at us and laugh.
How long do we have
To keep this car?
When are we getting a car
That we will be proud for
You to drive?

In the meantime . . .
Thank you, Mom
Because even when our friends need a ride
You provide them transportation to or from their homes
Sometimes both ways.
Their new cars stay parked and gassed
You drive our friends home after dark and
Never speak a word to complain or blame
Parents who make no effort to do the same
Every once in a while for some other
Struggling mother supporting her children's hopes and dreams.
We have a jalopy for a car, but it transports us and our friends
From where we are to
Where our prosperous future will begin
When we need to get away
From wherever we are
I thank God and you, Mom that
We have a car.

No One More Than Mother

Before I close the book
On the final chapters of my life
I want to take a look at
Many of the people it took
To get me to the summit
Upon which I stand today.
No other human touch
Has impacted my life as much
As the all-encouraging, unconditional love such
As I have received my whole life
From my precious mother.

Mother's love has healed
All the storms I've faced
Because she had strategically placed
My life into the care of her God.
She understood; she knew
That only prayer could do
Whatever I would need
To bring me through
Repeated dangers, toils, and snares
All the days of my life.

The God she gave to me
Saved me and made me see
That all things are possible
For anyone who believes.
Her acts of love are proof
That the God of love and truth
Exists and He lifts His children
Out of chaos and the miry clay.

She taught me about The Way, so
Even when I went astray
I knew how to find
My way back home.
The Welcome mat that sat
At the door of Mom's heart
Was a good place to start
To trust in the loving and forgiving
Power of The Heart of God.

Mom made me serve our God in church
Until I discovered the value of His worth.
What a wealthy treasure I now possess
Too much to measure its success
With bringing love, joy, peace, and happiness
To each passing decade, year, day!

Your truth demonstrated proof of His.
I learned He forgives by
Receiving your forgiveness.
Being forgiven relieves and releases me
From my guilt and
Tilts my lean more dependently onto
The Everlasting Arm.
Mother's love and faith have guided me to a place
Where my God's amazing grace has
Erased my fears and disgrace.
No other has shown me His Light
No other has taught me about doing what's right
No other has trained me to fight
The good fight of faith
More than you have, Mother.
No one more than Mother!

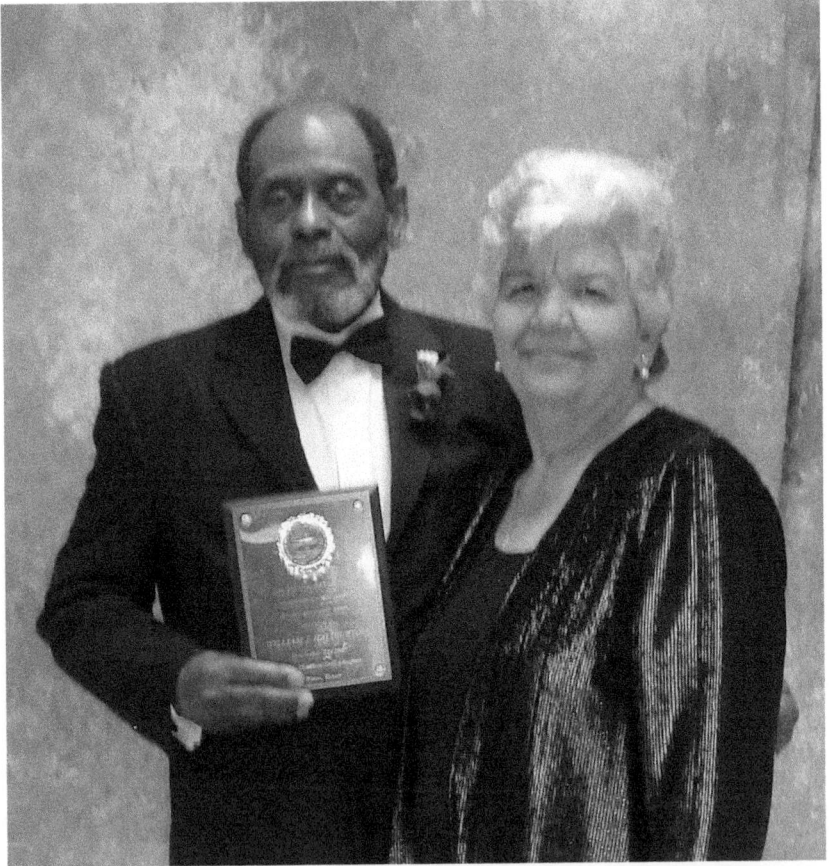

Daddy & Nattie

Daddy

Daddy's life, like Mama's life, unfolded into two volumes. Volume I includes all stories prior to meeting Natividad Pina. Volume II reveals his life with Natividad. We call her Nattie. She was Dad's second wife, with whom he had three children: Andrea, William, and David. A young William Franklin Haliburton was in love with the young woman he married, Delois Vonner. The middle-aged Will deeply loved and valued Nattie.

Nattie added years to my father's life. He once told me that God had given him a second chance. I understood what he meant by that statement based on the many conversations he and I had had throughout many years. Daddy was a far better husband to Nattie than he had been to my mother. Like most of us, he was a better man in his middle-aged years than he had been in his younger years. Therefore, although he had been a good father to my siblings and me, he was an even better father to his last three children than he had been able to be to his first six in our pre-teen and teenaged years.

Better is a relevant term. My father was a good father to the six of us. He loved us and cared for us. We knew his heart. We had his support. We were confident in his protection. He modeled before us Peter's instructions in 1 Peter 5:8, "Grow in grace." We watched a good man become a better one.

After I became an adult, I was exchanging niceties with an elderly woman, a neighbor from my childhood. Our paths had crossed while we were out shopping. In the conversation, she made a comment confessing her thoughts from earlier decades saying, "When your dad left your mom with all those girls," I was shocked and many responses to her rude remark flowed through my mind, but I chose not to disrespect her. I let her know that my dad had not left my mother and that my dad had been a lot more involved in our lives after my parents' divorce than outsiders knew. The busybody got the message.

When many of our peers graduated high school, their parents forced them to immediately survive on their own. They had no hope of parental support through college. The expectation was for these classmates to get out of their family homes and on their own. Both our mom and dad supported us through college.

Daddy bought Rita a white Gremlin, so she would have transportation while attending college at the University of Texas in Arlington. He bought Nita an olive green Pinto, so she would have transportation while attending Columbia College in Missouri. He bought me a royal blue Pinto. When the cars broke down, he either repaired them himself or paid to have them repaired.

I was riding around Waco with a friend one day when her car broke down. She was talking as if she were dumbfounded. I couldn't believe she didn't know what to do, so I told her what I would always do whenever I had car trouble. "Call your dad," I suggested. She did. When she got off the phone, I asked, "What did he say?" She said that he asked her, "What are you calling me for? Call a wrecker." I was shocked. She lived in the house with both her parents. He was a respected member of our community.

My dad would never have responded to any of his daughters, or sons for that matter, in that way. I had a deeper respect and appreciation for my dad. I could count on him whenever I needed him. My friend told me that she had only called her dad because I had suggested it. She knew he was not going to help her. She wished she had called a wrecker in the first place and not called her dad at all.

My parents divorced when I was eight years old. At that time, I had no idea the impact a divorce takes on a couple. I have since learned a great deal about it that puts into perspective both of my parents' behavior during those years. What I did understand at that time was life was so much better whenever Mama and Daddy kept their distance from each other. Although we all found ourselves facing "situational poverty" as a result of my parents' divorce, the peace the separation gave us all was worth it.

Daddy was reared in the West, Gerald, Abbott communities about fourteen miles north of Waco. He was child number six of seven. He was only two years old when his mother died. His oldest sister, Aunt Helen, was fourteen years old and his next oldest sister, Aunt Virgie, was twelve. Aunt Helen and Aunt Virgie altered the plans for their lives and committed themselves to caring for the little babies my grandmother had left behind in her death. I often refer to Aunt Helen's being the closest person to a grandmother my siblings and I knew.

Not only did these two little girls, Aunt Helen and Aunt Virgie, lose their mother at such a vulnerable age, but they also had been thrust into motherhood. Needless to say, my aunts spoiled my dad. The older he got, the more manipulative he became. He had their hearts until they were separated by death. They never denied him any request that was within their power. Aunt Helen never married and never had children of her own. Aunt Virgie eventually married and had five children, but I doubt that she spoiled any of them to the degree that she allowed my dad to have his way. Life with my mother taught Daddy the hard way that he would have to learn to cope with not always getting his way.

My mother frustrated my dad on many levels and areas of the life they lived together. They were married in 1951 when, as Archie Bunker put it, "Girls were girls and men were men." Husbands had clearly defined roles, and wives had clearly defined different roles. Unfortunately, for Mom and Dad's marriage, the defined roles for wives were losing their clarity. Mom was changing with the times, and Dad was fighting to maintain the traditional understanding of the role of the wife. Two Titanic wills collided, each for the most noble of reasons, and there was absolutely no chance of reconciliation between them. My mother had the courage to bring an end to the chaos that had become our lives.

My parents' divorce could be compared to corrective surgery. A body part that does not function properly can create pain and discomfort that may only worsen without surgery. The body part must undergo surgery. The recovery process is painful but progressively becomes less painful. The body part completely heals and no longer experiences pain. My parents' divorce healed us all.

Also in the 1950s and 1960s, America was evolving as a result of the Civil Rights Movement under the leadership of Dr. Martin Luther King Jr. Daddy was excited by what these changes meant to African Americans and to him and his life even in Waco, Texas. For him, life was as he had envisioned it and getting better. He had an attractive wife. He had a son, and he had five daughters. He was active in his church. He was actively involved in community work. He was buying his family a home. He provided his family transportation that we were proud for our parents to drive. He had a good job, and he had a good name.

While Dad was positioning himself to run for public office, Mom was positioning herself to achieve a goal of her own. In 1968, Daddy wanted to be elected the county commissioner of Precinct 3, and Mama wanted a divorce. He did not get his way. She did. My mother frustrated my dad.

My parents were married for seventeen years. They became increasingly civil toward each other over the decades that followed their divorce. In October 2010, my mother was in Washington, DC at the bedside of their son. She phoned my dad and said, "Our son is in trouble." On November 11, 2010, Dad called me in my hotel room on the day of Bruce's funeral. He asked, "Who is in the room with you?"

I answered, "Mama, Cheryl, Judy, and Nita." He said, "Tell everybody in the room I love them." I understood what that meant. It spoke volumes. Mom and Daddy had forgiven each other and were finally genuinely at peace with each other. It took five decades and Bruce's death to broker their truce.

Our family home was built on a corner lot. Behind our property was a small Baptist church named after our neighborhood, Carver Park Baptist Church. Most of the members lived within walking distance, so there was limited parking provided on the field that served the neighborhood children for football games and baseball games whenever church was not in session and dependent upon the season.

Carver Park Church also owned the lot directly across the street from our home. Every once in a while, the church would mow the grass in that field, but most times it was overgrown. It was larger than the field that served as the church's parking lot, so whenever it was mowed, the older kids in the neighborhood enjoyed sports activities there.

On one particular occasion, some middle school boys were engaged in a baseball game. Norman may have been a ninth grader. He was up to bat. He hit the ball beyond the field. The ball crossed the street and our yard in the air and landed only after crashing through the large picture window of our home. Bruce witnessed it and even made an effort to jump up and catch the ball but was unsuccessful with preventing the accident.

I remember thinking then about how angry Daddy was going to be, but he was not angry at all. Daddy spent more time in conversations with Bruce and others in the neighborhood about Norman's talent and the distance Norman had hit that ball than he spent talking about that broken window. Dad secured the window for the evening and slept in front of it on the living room couch that night. He and Bruce replaced the window the next day.

The location of our family home provided us considerably more privacy than most families expect to have in a neighborhood like ours. We were not closely surrounded by other people's homes. Our backyard was fenced in and Daddy had laid smooth concrete sidewalks around most of our property. We also had a concrete driveway. We learned to ride bicycles and to skate in our own yard. Other children enjoyed coming to our house to play because Daddy had designed our yard for his children to have a safe place to play. No other home in the neighborhood had as much concrete as ours.

I emphasize that our driveway and sidewalks were comprised of smooth concrete. Daddy had personally prepped it, poured it, and laid it. Ask any child who has ever tried to ride a bike, skate, play Jacks, hopscotch, jump rope, bounce a ball or even run safely on unleveled concrete how important smooth, leveled concrete is. The children who played at our house knew that there was something different about our sidewalks. Daddy had seen to their safety and aesthetic beauty.

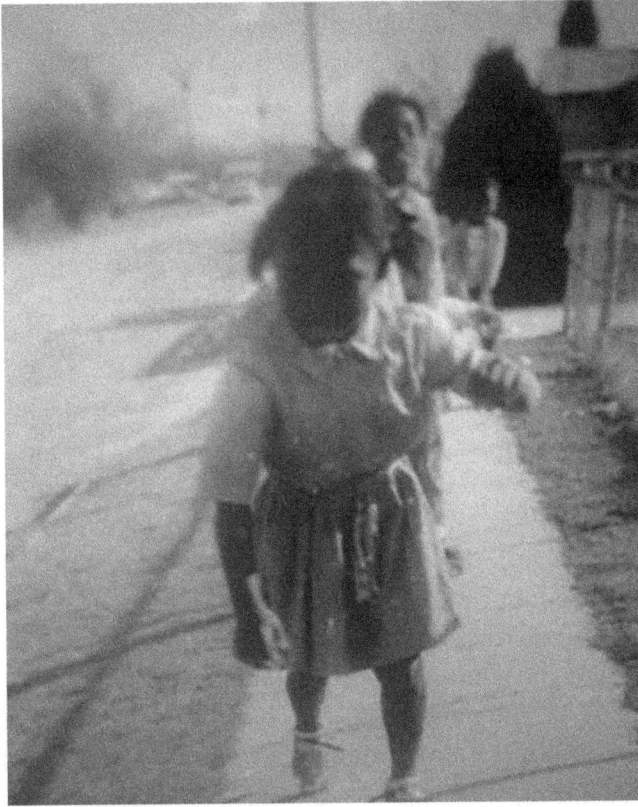

Margaret, a neighbor skating on our sidewalk

When I was about five or six years old, Cheryl and I were play-ing behind the family car in our driveway. Mom and Dad were both home and in the house. In those days, little children could play safely in their yards without close supervision. A parent's biggest fear was that their child may run out into the street and be accidentally hit by a passing car. Cheryl and I could be trusted not to go into the street, so my parents had no concerns about us being there alone.

Our neighbor's dog, King came into our driveway. Cheryl and I had no fear of dogs because we kept a family dog in our fence.

King was a large red Chow. As I recall the event, it seemed like King and I had looked each other eye to eye. He was panting, so I could see his black tongue. When Cheryl tells the story today, she says that King was leaving the driveway. He suddenly turned around as though he had forgotten something. I simply remember how painful it was when he bit me.

I headed toward the front door, screaming, "Daddy." I saw my dad jump off the porch rather than taking the steps. He was wearing a white T-shirt because he had been inside relaxing. In a matter of seconds, he had scooped me up into his arms. He took me into the house, handed me to my mother and told her to prepare me to go to the emergency room. Mom quickly cleaned me up and managed the bleeding.

A neighbor, Mr. Holbert, after finding out that I had been bitten by a dog, came into the house to check on my condition. Mom covered my naked body with a towel and allowed him to look at my wound. King had bitten a small chunk out of my upper lip.

I later learned that after handing me to my mother, Daddy got his shot gun and headed down the street to King's house. Mr. Holbert was driving by, saw my dad wearing a blood-soaked shirt and walking down the street carrying a shot gun and had decided to intervene. He had successfully stopped Daddy from shooting King on sight and had redirected Dad's attention to getting me some medical care. I got several stitches and ingested my meals through a straw for a few days. King was quarantined and monitored for rabies. He was given a clean bill of health and eventually returned home.

Daddy had a good job that paid him well and gave him access to great benefits and amenities. One of those benefits was affordable health care for the whole family. We received excellent health care. Judy had asthma, and it was necessary for her to have chronic care. Bruce's appendix ruptured, and he had to have surgery to remove it. Rita had rheumatic fever. I had to get stitches twice, once in my forehead and another time in my upper lip. I was hospitalized twice in an effort to treat me for epileptic seizures. Dr. Harry Slade treated me and said that I would outgrow them. He was right. I outgrew them. Cheryl had pneumonia as an infant. Mom was never hospitalized for illness, but she did benefit from the health care Dad provided because she had to maintain treatment for asthma.

Dad liked music, so we were all guided to appreciate music and to play musical instruments. We all played in our respective high school bands. Judy, Rita, Nita, Cheryl, and I played the flute. Bruce played the trumpet and the French horn. Among Dad's children with Nattie: Andrea played the French horn, Bill played the trombone, and David played the trumpet. My first five siblings and I, all sang in the age-appropriate choirs at church. Although Daddy never learned to play an instrument, he had a beautiful tenor voice.

We, children, would often gather around his chair and sing from a Baptist hymnal with him. In addition to church songs, we would sing the songs Dad taught us and songs that came over the radio. He loved Nat King Cole. Daddy piped music into our home like music in an elevator. I loved to hear him sing.

Every year, our family attended three major events that were unrelated to our church activities. One was the Heart of Texas Fair and Rodeo at the Coliseum in the white part of Waco. Daddy always purchased tickets to the rodeo. On our way into the rodeo, we would pass all of the fair activities. As children, we wanted desperately to ride the rides and play the games. We were never given the option. We bypassed the rides and games and went to the rodeo for years. We always enjoyed the excitement of the rodeo once there, but once Daddy stopped taking us to the rodeo, our interests in the rodeo also stopped.

A second annual family event we attended for years was at the YMCA. Daddy maintained a family membership with the Y. The Doris Miller YMCA was the African American branch. Every year they would host a family night. Some years we played bingo for prizes. I recall one particular year, Mr. Carey, the director showed a reel-to-reel movie. It was my first knowledge of Kurt Russell. The film, *Follow Me Boys*, starred Fred McMurray. It made an indelible, emotional impression on me.

The third annual event my family attended for years was The Genco Credit Union banquet. We would have dinner and then play bingo for prizes. Members of the credit union would participate in a business meeting. They would vote for and against people and policies. It was so boring to us as children but to play bingo was always worth the wait; win or lose. We had fun. I only remember winning once. My prize was a three-tier glass candy dish. I was so proud.

Daddy was a family man. He kept his children involved in wholesome activities. He encouraged us. He taught us to love the things he loved. I could probably speak for my siblings about whether or not he was successful with his efforts to direct what we learned to love from him, but I will only speak for myself. Daddy loved to travel. He loved to sing. He love to talk about the things that interested him such as history and politics. He loved learning. Most importantly, Daddy loved God, family and country, in that order. I have listed the things Daddy loved and succeeded in getting me to love too.

In the final years of his life, Daddy's vision rapidly diminished until he became totally blind. He gave up driving before his eightieth birthday. He stopped traveling and stayed close to home. He went to church as often as he could. He would attend Nattie's church for Sunday morning worship because it was convenient. She would take him to his own church Second Missionary Baptist Church, for first Sunday evening services, so he could participate in Communion. He continued sending his tithes to Second Baptist. He had been a faithful and active member for nearly five decades. Dad was proud of his pastor, Dr. Nika Davis who had been trained and reared in Christian education at Second Baptist his entire life.

On February 8, 2015, while my husband, Monty and I were in Frisco, Texas preparing to leave for church, Nattie called me. Daddy had been in and out of the hospital since November 2014 and was not improving. He told Nattie that he wanted to be placed on hospice and asked her to contact his children and other close loved ones. I notified Cheryl and Rita; Rita contacted Nita. I got on Interstate 35 and as fast as I could safely, raced to my dad's bedside. Cheryl called my cell. I asked her, "Does he know I'm coming?' She answered, "Yes." I spent my one hundred–mile-trip pleading with God not to let him die before I could get to him.

Daddy lived another thirteen days. Once again, I was forced to face the reality that the life of another loved one was set to terminate "any day now." On October 23, 2010, I left Bruce dying in Howard

University Hospital's Surgery Intensive Care Unit. At the time, I had no idea that he had only twelve days left to live.

My family and I had united in faith for Bruce's condition. We believed that he would recover. After all, we could not imagine life without him. We were incapable of thinking past the mere possibility that a time was approaching that we must face life without Bruce. What I did realize at that time was that Bruce was experiencing a closer walk with God.

Bruce and I had talked extensively about death and the dying process for years. We had both seen people on their death beds. As a minister, he had been with people at a closer point of death than I had been. His dear friend, Mike, was also a minister. Bruce walked closer through the dying process with Mike than he had with any other person. Bruce and Mike talked deeply on a variety of topics, death included. Bruce had expressed to me how disappointed he was that Mike had not shared more about the process of dying with him.

In 2006, I went to the bedside of my cousin, Peggy. She had chosen to die at home. Her daughter was giving her excellent care with the assistance of a hospice nurse. Peggy was precious to me. She and my oldest sister, Judy were the same age. On a photograph taken when they were about three months old, they look like twins. My mother had breastfed them both.

Peggy was a spoiled, military brat. She had lived in a variety of places and had had a variety of experiences far different from life in Waco. After graduating college, Peggy returned to Waco. It was then that I got to know her better. She was fun. She was exciting. She was full of wisdom. She cared and knew how to break through the layers teenagers use to shield their insecurities. She provided the guidance I needed from a big sister.

When I went to Peggy's bedside, she was obviously experiencing pain and discomfort. She taught me something crucial that I shared with Bruce shortly upon learning it. She said, "It's so hard."

I was curious and wanted to be clear. I knew that I could ask Peggy anything. I asked, "What's hard, Peggy?"

She answered, "Dying."

Concerned, I followed with, "The pain?"

Her response was, "No." My next guess was that she may have been talking about how hard it was for her to leave her children, but when I asked her, she indicated that she was not worried about them. She knew they would be fine. She explained that she was spiritually, emotionally, and psychologically ready to die, but her body just would not go on and die physically. Although I do not recall her exact words, I got her message. I do remember her words, "Dying is hard work." Peggy died the next day.

Bruce and I had shared our stories with each other. His was about Mike's experience and mine was about Peggy's. Psalm 139:14 says, "I will give thanks to You, for I am fearfully and wonderfully made." Peggy's message helped Bruce understand more clearly what he saw Mike experience but was unable or unwilling to articulate. Bruce and I had promised each other that if it were possible, whichever one of us was dying first would communicate the details of its beauty and glory to the other. The one dying would comfort the other who would continue living with the gift of understanding its spiritual process.

On October 23, 2010, I was leaving Bruce in Washington, DC, to return to Texas. My last conversation with Bruce triggered alarm bells within me. Rita and Cheryl had just flown in The City. Mama had ordered everyone to DC. She was led by the Spirit and obeyed without even knowing that Bruce would not survive.

Before leaving the hospital to catch my plane, I convinced Rita and Cheryl to make me a promise. I told them that if it looks like Bruce will not live, please minister to him differently. Rita broke down. She was not open to the thought. She was full of faith in God. She believed in the miraculous power of God's word. To think anything short of faith in a miracle was an act of treason to the King of kings. She only wanted to focus on faith for Bruce to live. I did not press my point; however, both Rita and Cheryl agreed to honor my request.

God is everything Rita believed and yet believes Him to be and more, despite the fact that Bruce died. It took faith in a God of miracles to endure the heartbreak of losing Bruce to death. In my weakness, I discovered His strength. He is able to carry us through.

Christians who are aware that they are dying have an opportunity to "give up the ghost." We must minister to them differently. We must not withhold the good news found in God's word that addresses death. Rather than avoiding the topic of death, we must speak of it until the one who is dying gets excited and welcomes the opportunity to transition from this life into eternal life with our Savior. The promises of the Resurrection from the Dead are the most crucial when one is facing death. The Word that speaks of eternal life refreshes and restores the soul, especially the soul trapped inside a doomed body struggling to die.

I went into Bruce's room to tell him goodbye. My last conversation with him was close to as follows:

Francene:	Are you afraid?
Bruce:	(He shook his head.) No. I am not afraid.
Francene:	Do you want to be moved? (Some of us doubted the quality of his care.)
Bruce:	No.
Francene:	I am leaving. I am returning to Texas. I am not coming back until you are ready to come. I will come and get you. If you need me to come back before then, just tell somebody to tell me. I will come back.

Bruce raised up from his bed as if powered by a sudden burst of energy, turned his face toward mine, looked me in my eyes and said, "I'll see you in Texas." He had the look he would give to assure people that he was giving his word. It was a look of assurance that comes from having a history of demonstrating integrity. His look spoke volumes. With tears streaming down my face, I put his right hand to my lips and kissed him goodbye. Twelve days later, Bruce transitioned fearlessly into life everlasting.

February 8, 2015, marked Day Number 13 in the countdown to the day Daddy died. We had all been summoned to say our goodbyes. Daddy had a dutiful wife who was at his bedside day and night. He had eight living children. We along with other dear relatives and friends were able to say our goodbyes and listen to him pass along his patriarchal wisdom. We ministered to him differently. We sang hymns of faith. We read and quoted scriptures with him and to him day after day and throughout the thirteen-day process. We wanted to build his faith, so God's word would bring him peace and comfort.

Dr. Nika Davis, Daddy's pastor came to visit him. Daddy spoke very directly with him about the particulars of his homegoing services. Dr. Davis ministered to him and prayed with him. Dying Saints appreciate the voice of their shepherd from the church where they lived their Christian lives.

Daddy was totally blind and unable to see. He had the Word of God committed to memory and hidden in his heart. He would call for certain scriptures, and someone would find the scripture and read it to him. Sometimes he would just quote the scripture alone. Other times he would quote a scripture as someone read it. He found comfort in the Word of God while he was gripped in the dying process. I created poems about the scriptures he quoted the most.

Daddy had the King James Version of the scripture committed to memory. His experience taught me that people who have spent decades finding comfort in the KJV of The Bible needed to use that same version as they wrestle in warfare on their death beds. They also need familiar songs that have seen them through the tough times in their lives. The number one contemporary Gospel song cannot compare to "Amazing Grace" and "What a Friend We Have in Jesus" when older warriors are fading off the scene and heading for their eternal rewards.

At first, Daddy was not as fearless in his dying process as Bruce had been. He would become upset and agitated. He made fruitless efforts to get out of bed. By these days, he was too weak to even stand. Nattie was so patient with him. She would talk to him and try to get him to relax and stay in bed. He would become frustrated with her because he felt she was keeping him from doing what he wanted to do. Indeed, she was, but it was for his own good. She loved him. Deep within, he knew that. In fact, he had spent the second half of his life depending on her love for him. I repeat, Nattie added years to my dad's life. Her love made life worth living for him.

Monty was working in Dallas and living in our Frisco house. I was still working in Waco and living through the week in our Waco home. On Fridays, I would drive to Frisco and spend the weekend with Monty. During Daddy's last thirteen days, I took Family Medical Leave (FMLA) from my job. I went to the hospital through the week rather than to work. On Friday evenings (February 13 and 20), I left the hospital and went to Frisco. On his last Sunday, I returned to Waco and went back to the hospital and prepared for the next week.

On Sunday, February 15, while sitting in church, I heard someone sing the words to Tis So Sweet To Trust In Jesus. The words refreshed me. I knew that was the song Daddy needed to hear. By the time I arrived to his bedside, he was upset and having one of his anxiety attacks. He spoke to me as if I did not understand the challenge before him. He said, "I'm dying, Fran." I responded gently, "I know, Daddy." For some strange reason only known to God, I spoke words that made sense to Daddy and to me.

I said with such certainty, "But there's a garden." In that instant, he settled and lay back in his bed.

I love the words, "There's a garden where Jesus is waiting." They are the opening words to a song with other words that I don't know. I never learned the words because I could never get passed the joy of knowing that Jesus is waiting. Daddy found peace in remembering that Jesus is waiting. I held him in my arms and sang the tune I had planned.

Tis so sweet
To trust in Jesus
Just to take Him at His word
Just to rest upon His promise
Just to know Thus saith the Lord.
Jesus, Jesus
How I trust Him
How I've proved Him o'er and o'er
Jesus, Jesus
Precious Jesus
O for Grace
To trust Him more.

The peace of God surpasses all understanding. Jesus is our Prince of Peace (Philippians 4:7). Christians recognize, respect and respond to His presence. Revelation 14:13 records, "And I heard a voice from Heaven saying unto me, Write, Blessed are the dead which die in the Lord from henceforth: Yea, saith the Spirit, that they may rest from their labours; and their works do follow them." The warriors of God face death differently when they know that they are dying in the Lord.

Daddy

Singing with Daddy

Sing with me, Daddy, and
Teach me the magic music gives.
Each word lives
In the rhythm and the beauty of
Your tenor voice.
I rejoice at every
Chance to sing with you.
Thank you, Daddy, for
The joy that music brings
For the gift you shared
Each chance we've had to sing.
I cannot express to you
How much it really means.
But I'll say thank you, Daddy
To you anyway
For the love of music
That I feel each day
For the magic that I feel
Each time I sing
For the memories of
The times I sang with you.
Thank you!

Daddy Speaks of Love

When the man of God
I call Daddy speaks of love,
I know that he is thinking of
You and me.
When he meditates and consecrates
His spoken words in worship to God.
I know that he is still teaching
You and me
What is most important even
When life gets hard.

"Charity suffers long and is kind"
Crosses his mind as he suffers
Pain and discomfort.
As he bears all things from
His bed of affliction,
He yet hopes all things with the
Same conviction that he has
Always hoped since the days
When he was young and
His body was strong.

"And now abide faith, hope, and charity:
These three."
He repeats the Word to assure
You and me
That having faith and hope are great
But having charity is the greatest of the three
For God, our Creator, is Love.
When Daddy speaks of love
He's thinking about you and me and eternity.

Daddy Still

Daddy on Earth
Daddy in Heaven
Three wait while
The eight who remain
Hear your voice
See your face and
Feel the embrace
of a father's love.
When God decides
You will abide forever
with Edwin, Roberta, and Bruce
Still fit for the Master's use.
Whether in Heaven or
on Earth
You will be Daddy still.

My Hero

The first hero I ever knew
Always rescued me
Until I grew
Old enough and
Smart enough and
Tough enough
Then wise enough
To know that
My first hero
Would be the only hero
I would ever need.
For my first hero taught me about
My everlasting hero, Jesus.
So
Thank you, Daddy!

Secure with Daddy

In the arms of my daddy
When I was a little girl
I learned to feel
Safe and secure
Despite the evil in the world.
I felt the same assurance
While gripping one of
His large strong hands
Clean and smooth in
Their appearance
As I tagged along on errands.
The people that we greeted
Seemed to always be
Respectful of and delighted
To see my dad and me.
The hands and arms
That kept me safe
So many years ago
Are still controlled
By Daddy's heart of love
That made them work just so.

Strong in the Lord

Weak translates to strong
to those of us who belong
to the King of Glory.
Daddy is strong in the Lord
and in the power of God's might.
Every hour Daddy heals
as he yields all his cares
for Jesus to bear.
When Daddy lifts his head from prayer
he speaks of strength
instead of a body that has been led
to rebel against the Ancient of Days.
Our thoughts are not God's thoughts.
Our ways are not God's ways.
And though Dad may seem weak
it is then that God's Word says that
he is strong.

Strong in the Power of His Might

Being physically strong
is not so important
when things start going wrong
with your body
once Time begins to take its toll.

Being strong in the Lord
will see you through
the long haul of life
whether young, seasoned, or old.

The power of His might will hold out
when your grip is weak and it is no longer
necessary for your feet to touch the ground.

The power of His might makes
you stronger than ever because
you have never needed Him
like you need Him now and
He is here.

To know Him and feel Him near
is to feel the power of His might
and to know that you are stronger
than ever
Even though your body is no longer young.

The Whole Armor

While lying in a hospital bed
Daddy remains dressed from head
to toe, ready for battle against
any spiritual foe
who dares to draw near.

While in the doctors' care
the wounded warrior prepares daily
to war against the wiles of the enemy.
With legs unable to stand,
Daddy stands at his Master's command.
The gospel of peace cover his feet.

Fiery darts lay around his room
unable to wound the warrior
wielding the shield of faith.

The helmet of salvation protecting his head
welcomes the truth instead of the lies
the devil tells strong men
warring with weak bodies.

The blood of Jesus will never fail, so
no fiery dart from Hell can penetrate Daddy's
breastplate of righteousness.

Hidden deep within Daddy's heart is
the part of God's armor that is sharp enough
to separate soul from the Spirit.
Those who hear it, who hear the Word of God
are strong enough to move mountains.

Dressed for battle both day and night
Daddy's light shines.
He is strong.
He is armed.
He is unharmed and comforted by
the Chief Shepherd's rod.
Daddy rests,
dressed in the whole armor of God

In the Beginning

Dad can be heard saying
"In the beginning was the Word and
The Word was with God and
The Word was God,"
while lying in a hospital bed.
He is led by the Spirit living within
To begin and end his meditations
Remembering the Author and Finisher
of his faith.
All through the day
Before each meal.
You will hear him quote
The words John wrote
To begin his book.

Look Up, Daddy

Look up, Daddy
Lift those eyes that no longer see
In honor of the God, who will forever be
Your Provider, Deliverer, Savior
Your Lord.

Look up and listen for your name.
Soon He will come to claim you
As His child.
Soon
You will have unspeakable joy
While those who love and surround you today
Will mourn and pray for mercy.
We will survive the pain of unmeasured loss
When you cross over into Eternity.

Today, Daddy
Look up.
Open the gate to your heart.
Welcome the King of Glory.
The Author will soon finish your story.
Soon your name will be called, so, Daddy,
Look up.

The Haliburtons in 1968

Judy

Judy was seven years older than me. Her physical characteristics had my admiration, but I despised the mean-spirited person I perceived her to be. She was unnecessarily cruel in the ways she used to mistreat her younger siblings. She was never physically abusive, but she was mentally abusive. Fortunately, it was within an acceptable range common to the way younger siblings are treated by older siblings.

Judy became a teacher. She was exceptional in her knowledge of content, but she struggled in her classroom relationships just as she had made us struggle in our relationships with her as siblings. I have always declared that she acts as if she does not like children. Children are far from perfect, but Judy never seemed to realize that. She was always in conflict with her less-than-perfect students in my opinion.

My siblings and I loved her, and we knew she loved us too. After our parents divorced in 1968, Judy went to work, assisting my mother with supporting her younger siblings financially. We all found ourselves in situational poverty as a result of the divorce. The finances once used to support one household, suddenly had to support two households. To add complications to my dad's finances, he had to find a way to pay the debt he had incurred after he had lost his race for county commissioner. Every penny in both homes had been spoken for.

Judy worked as an operator for Southwestern Bell Telephone Company. One of my favorite memories about those years sums up what Judy meant to us younger sisters. It happened one summer day in the early 1970s. Rita, Nita, Cheryl, and I were home all day the summer months. Many parents have discovered that children eat more groceries when school is out for the summer months. We were no exception. Mom left for work during early morning hours and would not be home until into the evenings. Judy would also be at work.

It was past lunch time and the four of us: Rita, Nita, Cheryl, and I had held a discussion about being hungry and about trying to decide what to do about it. There was literally nothing in the house to cook or even to eat period. Rita and Nita busied themselves with other affairs even though the discussion had not produced a solution. Cheryl and I were alone. I had an idea.

The thought never crossed anybody's mind to call Mom's job. That was unthinkable. However, Judy was an operator. She was in the business of managing phone calls. Cheryl and I agreed that we should call Judy's job, and so we did. We laugh about it today, but it warms my heart still when I think of the little girls who believed they would be all right if they could just get a message to their big sister. Before we gave up on the operator and hung up on her, I was able to ask one question before it became obvious that we had a failing plan. I said to the operator, "Hello. May I please speak to Operator Judy?" The operator must have thought it was a prank.

It was the hungriest I ever remember being, yet I don't remember what it felt like. I just recall the emotional memories attached to the experience. We survived the day. Mom came home, and we went grocery shopping. Judy got a big laugh. She was still our hero. We believed that if Mama couldn't, Judy could. (I still thought she was mean and didn't like less-than- perfect children.)

Judy graduated high school in 1970 from a segregated African American public school. She chose to remain in Waco and get a college degree from Baylor University. Rather than going away for college like her many classmates, Judy stayed in Waco, so she could continue to help my mother financially provide for the four girls who still needed to get out of high school and out on their own.

One of my classmates, Donald who was also a neighbor shared a story with me about Judy's impact on his life many years after its occurrence. Donald was our "class clown." He was tall and slender like J. J. Walker, a character from the television series, *Good Times*. Donald dressed like J. J. and wore a white cap like J. J.'s, and he was just as funny as J. J.

Donald claims in his story that one day he was outside playing, minding his own business while his mother was in the house reading the local newspaper. He said she came to the door and called him inside with that Mama voice that means you had done something wrong; you were caught, and now you were in trouble. Once Donald got inside, his mother opened the newspaper and asked him, "Why can't you do that?" Judy's name was in the paper because she had been recognized as a graduate of Baylor University.

Donald read the article and answered his mom's question. He told her okay. He would go to college, but first he would get out of elementary school. (The truth is that when Judy graduated Baylor, we were in the tenth grade. My comedic friend's twist on the story put him in elementary school.) We were adults when Don shared his story of the impact Judy's accomplishment not only had in my home, but also in his home.

Judy and I were the only career teachers among the six of us. Nita taught at a private Catholic school for a year and decided that she was not meant to teach. Nita made the right decision because if she found teaching private Catholic school students a challenge, she would never have survived teaching urban public school students.

Judy barely did. The teaching profession kept changing the rules of engagement, and it became increasingly difficult for behavior and expectations of a stubborn, set-in-her-ways teacher to operate within the guidelines of change. She stuck out like a sore thumb. She was unable or unwilling to develop the new skills necessary to teach the challenging students who had begun attending the public schools. She finally conceded, but it was not until she had set her last bridge in her teaching career ablaze and watched it go up in flames.

Big Sister

The big sister loves to boss
The siblings small enough to be tossed
Helplessly and hopelessly aside.
Crushing the little one's pride
Becomes sport,
Sort of a game
Designed to master and tame
The little one's will before
He/She develops the skills to resist
Big Sister Demands.
Big sister's hands
Once used to hit
Would later work to get
The younger his/her heart's desire
Big sister's tongue, that
Once wagged to boast and brag
That she had permission and
Power to do with you
As she pleased,
Would later plead your cause and
Place many, many calls
To provide you gifts and peace.
Because she paid the cost
To assure no long term loss
To the young one's hopes and dreams
The big sister who seemed
To love to boss
Is seen as the one
Who loves
Like a boss.

Bruce

✦ ✦ ✦ ✦ ✦ ✦

Birthday season and the holiday season gave the Haliburton Family a lifetime of excitement. Judy's birthday was August 5. Labor Day was in September. Bruce's birthday was October 20. Halloween/trick-or-treat was October 31. Francene's birthday was November 2, and Daddy's was November 12. Thanksgiving was later in November. The twins' birthday was December 8. Christmas was December 25. A week later was New Year's Day, January 1. Mom's birthday was January 3.

For decades, we spent six months of every year celebrating family milestones. (Cheryl's birthday, April 23, was within the six months of a slightly-less exciting season of celebrations such as Easter, Mother's Day, and Father's Day.)

The events of 2010, during the Haliburtons' Celebration Season, unfolded a timeline of sorrow.

October 7: Bruce notified me that he had stomach cancer.

October 16: Bruce had surgery that revealed that his life expectancy was limited to months.

October 18: Bruce aspirated in recovery after the surgery for a chemotherapy port.

October 20: Bruce spent his fifty-seventh birthday in ICU, struggling for the limited months left in his life.

November 2: Francene received a call on her fifty-first birthday that Bruce may not survive the night.

November 3: Bruce died.

November 10: The Haliburtons from Texas traveled to Washington, DC, for Bruce's funeral.

November 11: Bruce's Homegoing Celebration was held at Mt. Olive Baptist Church in Arlington, Virginia, and his remains were interred in Maryland soil.

November 12: The Texas Haliburtons returned to Texas. It was Daddy's seventy-ninth birthday.

November 13: A Memorial Celebration for Rev. Dr. Bruce Earl Haliburton was held at Second Missionary Baptist Church in Waco, Texas, so that the friends and family of the Haliburton Family who were unable to attend the Virginia services could share and express their condolences.

November 25: Thanksgiving Day was our family's first holiday after Bruce's death. We soldiered on with faith in 1 Thessalonians 5:18, "In everything give thanks . . ."

In 1956, at the age of three, Bruce got his first job. My parents had twins: Rita and Nita. Our oldest sister, Judy, was a fragile, four-year-old asthmatic, so Bruce strapped on a diaper bag full of survival supplies for two. By the time Cheryl and I came along, Bruce was well-established in his role as "big brother, champion, and super-hero." We adored him.

From our father, Bruce learned to be a godly man, full of integrity. It was Daddy who taught him that men should be strong. (Bruce was strong. He was an athlete.) It was from Daddy that he learned to be the provider, protector, counselor, and adviser that he became to his own children: Tiffany and Troy.

From our mother, he learned to sacrifice his personal interests in exchange for bringing joy and pleasure to those he loved. By example, my mother taught him to pick his battles and to "follow peace." (Bruce was a man of peace.) Because of his mother, Bruce did not find strong, independent, opinionated women strange. Because of his father, he did not fear them.

From the late, great Dr. Leon Fernandez Hardee, the pastor of our childhood, he learned the importance of being a "teaching shepherd." Men of God, called to be teachers, are patient. They draw illustrations that give clarity to God's word. Like all good teachers, Bruce was patient.

Bruce arrived in Washington, DC, in 1976 and remained there for thirty-four years with these values, and many more, packed in his character. It was his heritage, as well as the heritage of Judy, Rita, Nita, Francene, and Cheryl given to us by our parents and the church of our childhood. I believe even Bruce's enemies would agree, that his passion for justice and righteousness made him a relentless and formidable foe. Bruce would never give up.

The summer of 1969, Daddy took Bruce, Rita, Nita, Cheryl, and me on vacation to our first trip to Washington, DC. Daddy loved history and politics, and he made history lovers of each of us. I loved DC. for its historical significance, but more importantly for becoming a part of my family history while there on vacation. We were so excited that Daddy had let Bruce (who at that time was sixteen years old) drive.

During that same vacation, we also went to New York. Bruce was thrilled to drive across the Brooklyn Bridge until Daddy had everybody look out the right side window in order to view the Statue of Liberty. Keeping his eyes on the road in the heavy traffic, Bruce cried out in panic, "Daddy, I can't see." Daddy took the wheel while Bruce leaned forward, turned his head away from the traffic, and caught a glimpse of Lady Liberty. Then he smiled that smile that those of us who knew him remember.

Bruce developed several effective ministries while serving God in Washington, DC. The Christian education he received at First Baptist Church under the late, great Dr. Leon Fernandez Hardee prepared him for God's call. His Christian education drove him to always be found trying to "help somebody as he passed along." Bruce's motto was always "Others."

I loved Washington, DC, as a child because of its historical significance. I loved it even more later because that was where Bruce was. I learned to love Heaven as a child because my parents, Papa Hardee, and my First Baptist family taught me to love it. I learned to love Heaven even more as my desire grew to spend eternity with Jesus. Now that Bruce has made Heaven his home, words cannot express the depth of love I have for Heaven. I can't imagine "his smile" the moment I see him there.

91

Whenever members of our family travel away from home, we always make contact upon returning home. Before we learned to use texting, this task was completed with a brief phone call. Bruce had visited us in Texas in August of 2010. He had performed the marriage ceremony for Nita's son, Steven and his bride, Lauren. He sent me a two word text message upon returning to Washington, DC.

Some months after Bruce's death, I was scrolling through my text messages. I saw his name in my contacts and decided to look at past communications between us. I opened his last message to me. It read, "Home safe." Indeed you are, Bruce.

Keep Laughing

Even though you know that I am gone,
You still desire to rush home
To tell me the latest news.
Come on and tell me anyway.
I'll be waiting, watching, and listening

For the excitement in your voice
As you share the story of your choice.

When you laugh,
I will laugh too,
The same way we laughed
When neither of us cared
Who thought we looked and sounded foolish.

Our loved ones loved watching
The exchange of laughter between us.
For the laughter between you and me

Healed us all.
Do you recall
How we would still away,
Leaving them folded over,
Slayed in the wake of our exhaust?

Keep laughing and baffling
Those who wonder why it seems
You never laugh alone.
I am laughing with you still,
Even though I am gone.

Fran and Bruce share a laugh

My Altar

Don't stand too close while you're laughing,
For I have built the Lord an altar near my bed, and
Only those who are led by the Spirit

Should approach as the final grains of sand

Mark the days of my life.
For the time of my departure is at hand, and
God is present listening to my prayers and to
The prayers of those intervening for me.
I have no more time for the folly we once shared,

Folly that seemed to bind our hearts and minds and
Synchronize our souls.
For He who said, "All souls are mine," is present

To bind my soul forever with His and
To take me away, and
I want to go in peace.
So don't stand too close to my altar
If you have no prayer to offer
The God I am about to meet.

Think of Jesus

Think of Jesus when you think of me,
For He and I are here together
Thinking of you.
Where I am now,
I see and know more than
I ever knew before.
Think of Jesus when you think of me.
There is no other way
For you to imagine my joy.
Think of Jesus when you think of me.
We are watching when tears flow from your eyes.
Whether in joy or pain,
Your days of sunshine or days of rain,

Jesus and I are both watching.
So think of Jesus every time
You take the time to think of me.
He's made me greater now
Than I ever was before.
I now know more than you may think I know, and
I haven't missed a thing.
So, think of Jesus every day that
You think of me.
For there is no other way
For you to know my joy.

Rita and Nita

Rita Kay and Nita Fay are twins. I always took pride in the fact that my family had a set of twins. It made me feel that my family was unique. I considered it as the high-flying banner that refuted any doubt that my family was special.

According to both my parents, as toddlers, Rita and Nita created a language that they used in private conversations between themselves. I suspect the communication challenge was Rita's since she served as the bilingual interpreter among Nita and all others in their world. As twins, they were always together, so Nita had little to no need or request to communicate without her interpreter. Rita was able to ask for whatever they wanted.

My parents often shared stories reflecting their "modus operandi." Rita was the brain and the boss, and Nita was the muscle and enforcer. Rita would introduce them to strangers. Rita would say, "Hi. My name is Rita. She's Nita. We're twins. I'm the oldest, but she's the biggest."

When they were quite small, the twins decided it would be fun to play with fire. It was during the cold winter season. My parents would warm the home of our childhood with Dearborn heaters. One of the twins stuck a sock into the fire of one of those heaters. (They were so young when the incident happened that neither of them remembers which of them set the sock on fire; however, they do recall the incident.)

My mother, listening from another room, could hear Rita saying repeatedly to Nita, "Stomp it," followed by the sound of a tiny foot stomping the wooden floor. Mom was so surprised to see the small blaze on the floor. She knew the twins needed to be watched; she was learning how closely they needed to be watched. On another occasion, the twins tried to broil a hairbrush while Mom was cooking dinner in the oven.

The twins had trouble and caused trouble because they would not go on to sleep when it was their bedtime. While all others in the family slept, the twins would get up and watch television until midnight. Prior to the 1970s, there were only three major television networks: CBS, ABC, and NBC, and they all stopped broadcasting at midnight. Everyone in America turned their televisions off and silenced the annoying sound that indicated the networks were no longer broadcasting.

Daddy decided to teach the twins a lesson. He was going to succeed where Mom had failed. His plan was to watch television with them until their bedtime. He was going to put them to bed. If they were to get out of bed and make an attempt to watch television after being put to bed, he was prepared to deal with them. Daddy would in later years tell in the story that he heard the little voices of the twins calling to him, "Daddy. Wake up, Daddy. It's time to go to bed. The television's gone off. Wake up, Daddy."

That night the twins taught Daddy a couple of lessons. One of which was not to be so sure that he could do with the twins what Mama could not do. The twins were a dynamic duo. Even at a young age, they understood that they were more powerful when they worked together. They functioned and accomplished their goals in tandem for decades.

In 1975, the twins graduated high school. Rita attended the University of Texas in Arlington, and Nita headed north to Columbia College in Missouri. Finally, we were all liberated by their separation

Judy and Bruce holding the twins, Rita and Nita

The Twins

The Twins each have names.
They are not the same person
Poured into two vessels.
They wrestled their way
Out of the womb
One at a time
Only to find a world
Full of people, constantly
Trying to keep them confined and
Combined as two halves
Creating one whole.
One day,
They broke the mold and
The yoke they had worn for years
Shattered and
Each became free to chase
What mattered in her own heart.
Apart, they accomplished so much more
Yet seemingly still attached
Just as before by
An invisible, umbilical
Cord of Love.

Cheryl

I referred to her in later years as "my first baby." Cheryl was my parents' last child together. I was only seventeen months older than her. We were nearly the same size. People who knew that my parents had twins would mistake the two of us as The Twins. Cheryl and I were so close in age that her arrival forced me to relinquish my amenities as Mommy's baby before I was ready.

Mom tells a story about a time when she was holding Cheryl, a newborn, in her arms. I approached them with particular interest in the baby. Mom had taught me to kiss the baby's feet. (Mom still has concerns about the germs that can be transferred by kissing a baby's face or hands. Babies put their hands in their mouths.) While Mom's attention was focused on her baby's face, I focused mine on the baby's feet, more specifically on Cheryl's little toe. Mom thought I was kissing the little princess's feet, but I was actually biting her toe.

Cheryl's red face and squeal alerted Mom, and she saw me bearing my teeth into Cheryl's toe just in time. Mom says she knocked me upside my head so hard that I landed in the safe arms of Granddaddy, Dad's father, who had moved quickly to my rescue. All of my earliest memories of Cheryl are of her being in my protective custody against all of her enemies, so I found this story fictional and entertaining. However, it is true.

Bruce was allowed to name Cheryl. He had a "puppy-love" crush on a smart little girl in his first grade class. Her name was Cheryl Munson. It was important to spell the baby's name just like Cheryl's with a C and not an S. Although nothing ever developed from Bruce's crush on Cheryl, like Wimp, Cheryl Munson became Bruce's lifelong friend.

Bruce, Cheryl, and Wimp all went away to college together at North Texas State University. Cheryl met and married a guy named Vincent. Whenever Bruce and his wife, Brenda, were in Texas, they would visit Cheryl and Vincent in Houston.

In 1985, Bruce was visiting in Texas. The Twins were expected for a visit as well. Cheryl Haliburton was attending the University of Texas in Arlington and was expected home to spend time with the family while the six siblings could be together. Cheryl's arrival was later than expected, and she was not answering the incremental phone calls in our efforts to reach her.

I was in the kitchen washing dishes when the house phone rang. This was before the time of cell phones. Rather than everyone receiving calls on their individual devices like now, family members shared a landline. The person calling would have to ask to speak to the person for whom they were calling. Any family member was free to answer the home phone. It was not considered an invasion of one's privacy. Since Bruce was closest to the phone, he answered it.

The conversation I heard was one-sided. Bruce said, "Hello. *(There was a brief pause while he listened.)* Cheryl is dead?" Bruce hung up the phone and came into the kitchen. All in the house had heard the words, "Cheryl is dead," so we gave Bruce our undivided attention. We were in shock and struggling to process what had been said. In less than a minute's time, we were trying to reconcile our future and whatever details Bruce was about to share regarding his statement, "Cheryl is dead?"

I remember what I was thinking in those seconds that seemed like an hour.

He said, "Cheryl is dead?" It sounded like a question. That means the caller was not sure. It could be a mistake.
There is time to pray for this not to be true. Once I hear the details, I'll pray and decide what to do next. We have not been able to find Cheryl, but we have not tried hard enough. We will

leave no stone unturned until we find Cheryl and solve this mystery.

Bruce felt the loss more deeply than the rest of us. The caller was an overwhelmingly upset Wimp. All he had said was, "Bruce, Cheryl Munson is dead" and had hung up the phone. We were sorry that Bruce had lost his friend, but we were extremely relieved and grateful to God that our Cheryl (my first baby) was not dead.

Cheryl and Francene

Sister

Be my lifelong friend.
Spend your time here
Loving me and supporting me
Through the good, bad, and ugliness
Within the days of my life.
You light the path
That brings me joy.
You no longer annoy me.
You help me feel and see
The power love possesses.
Your forgiveness is
The prize that drives my guilt away.
God may have made us sisters, but when
You became my lifelong friend
It was my choice.

Dr. and Mrs. L. F. Hardee (Leon Fernandez and Johnnie Dee)

First Baptist Church, National Baptist Convention (NBC)

I am, above all else without measure, proudest that I am a Christian. I do not boast in being a Christian because of any good or great thing that I have accomplished with my life. The only credit I can take in this most highly favored position in which I have found myself is that I made the right decision when I chose Christianity as the guide for my belief system. I thank God that I was born to parents who were Christians. By the time I was capable of comprehending the apologetics of Christianity, I only had to agree to the truths I had been taught by my father and my mother. It was not necessary for me to unlearn false doctrine(s).

I received my Christian education at First Baptist Church, NBC, under the leadership of Dr. Leon Fernandez Hardee and his beautiful, dutiful wife, Johnnie Dee Waters Hardee. He had been president of a defunct Christian college called Butler College, and she was an elementary school teacher. They were both well-educated and trained educators. They transferred their academic teaching skills and became specialists as Christian educators. I developed my belief system in a progressively methodical, age-appropriate environment. I have survived a lifetime of challenges using the biblical compass I was given as a child trained in the L. F. Hardee School of Christian Development. What a blessing!

We committed scripture to memory every week for years. We memorized the words and tunes to songs we sang in fellowship settings. We learned Bible stories that sometimes emphasized characters while at other times events were emphasized. The Bible was personally relevant because we were encouraged to apply what we were learning in our daily lives. We participated in making public presentations and reports. We were given these opportunities fifty-two Wednesdays a year, year after year. These opportunities were also provided twice every Sunday in those same years, in Sunday school and in Baptist Training Union.

David wrote in Psalm 119:105, "Thy word is a lamp unto my feet and a light unto my path." Truly, God's word has been that kind of guide in my life. My belief system has kept my life full of joy despite what was happening in my life. My belief system has kept me grounded through my life's highs and lows. My belief system has kept me in control when I was angry, as well as when I desired to behave selfishly. My belief system has kept me out of jail, out of harm's way and out of a psychiatric ward.

My belief system taught me to pray, and the God of my belief system convinced me that there is power in prayer. My belief system taught me that there was a God who loves unconditionally, but it was the God of my belief system who convinced me by His involvement in my life that He loves me unconditionally. God loves me. No one or nothing can ever change what my belief system has taught me about the God of my belief system. I learned His story. I learned how to please Him. I learned to trust Him. First Baptist Church, NBC taught me what I needed to know in order to personally get to know the God of my belief system, and what I learned has and will sustain me for the remainder of my life. I shall never thirst again.

My belief system educators taught me that the God of the system is omniscient, omnipresent, and omnipotent. They also taught me that I was accountable to the God of the system for my behavior and the choices I make in life. What a treasure I am convinced my belief is! The God of the system has been my guide through life's challenges.

The God of my belief system was interwoven throughout every aspect of my life. He was in my home. He was in my school as well as in my church. The God of my belief system was acknowledged and honored at the Girl Scout functions, the Boy Scout functions, at the YMCA at the annual Genco Credit Union banquet and at the Heart of Texas Rodeo. The God of my belief system was present everywhere my family and I went. He was an essential member of my family. I felt as responsible for being accountable to God as I felt being held accountable to my parents.

I am increasingly concerned about the large number of children growing up in homes without an honorable belief system. These children lack the guidance that a belief system provides. If they are also being reared by irresponsible parents and guardians of ignoble character, these children lack the security that limitations afford. They steal from others and harm others without remorse. Hurt people hurt others. Nowhere is this more prevalent in children's behavior than its presence in our public schools. Who is inflicting harm on these children and causing them to want to harm others? A belief system could end the cycle of paying pain forward.

Parents realize the value of providing their children academic educational opportunities, even if they themselves never took advantage of opportunities that were given to them. In fact, many of these parents struggle and sacrifice for their children's opportunities in order to save their children from making the same mistakes they made in wasting their educational opportunities.

I wish that parents would pursue a Christian education for their children with that same fervor and zeal. Whether or not the parents themselves go to church, I wish they would commit to getting their children to church. I encourage parents to acknowledge the importance of giving their children a belief system and then seeing to it that it develops to a level of maturity that can sustain their children's lives through their tough times. Tough times will come.

Children develop belief systems in various places. I recommend that parents intentionally determine the what, the where, the when, the who and the how regarding that development. A belief system can be developed strictly in the home. It can be developed in the school. It can be developed on the streets, at the Boys' Club, the YMCA or at some after school program or other organization. As a Christian, I recommend that parents search for the best possible church environment to develop their children's belief system, a church whose doctrine is supported by the Holy Bible.

I presently have a dear friend and colleague who is a Muslim. She is as devout to her belief system as I am to mine. As close as we have become, I doubt that I could dissuade her from what she believes, and I have no doubt that she cannot convince me to abandon my Christian beliefs in order to embrace the Koran. Oddly enough, we each believe that the God of our belief systems intentionally yoked our lives and our hearts together for a season.

I love the glory God gets from my fellowship with her. I have a Bible story/lesson for every challenge in my life. My belief system, combined with my teaching skills, has blessed me with the ability to make connections between my problems and biblical solutions. I pray to the God of my belief system, and I teach others to trust Him using that same method. With my precious Muslim friend, I tell her the Bible stories, but I do not insult her with offering her a Christian prayer. (Out loud, that is.) She is on my prayer list and when she faces particular challenges, I pray for her with laser precision. I love hearing her praise reports, and I love giving God the glory for His work. He manifests His presence and delivers.

My belief system taught me that if I wanted to enjoy life, I had to treat people the way I wanted to be treated. Luke 6:31 says, "And as ye would that men should do to you, do ye also to them likewise." The God of my belief system provided guidelines, so I could know the best way a person should be treated. Those godly guidelines, my parents and experiences in life taught me to value those guidelines above the many other false teachings I would encounter throughout my lifetime. Violations of those guidelines are extremely unattractive when displayed in human behavior. It is difficult to recognize the ugliness of those violations in our own behaviors but easily recognizable in the behaviors of others.

I hate feeling as though I am being judged by others, even when I agree with their judgment. Jesus teaches us in Matthew 7:1, "Judge not, that ye be not judged." This scripture helps me remember to focus on recognizing the ugliness of those guideline violations in my own behavior rather than focusing on the violations of others.

When I am at my best in treating others the way I would like to be treated, I am obeying the guidelines provided by the God of my belief system. Besides not judging others, I've learned to treasure many other guidelines for life, especially the entire thirteenth chapter of 1 Corinthians. Learning to love as instructed by the God of love is the best way to learn how to treat others the way one wants to be treated.

My parents saw to it that my siblings and I developed a belief system built on sound doctrine. My Christian faith has sustained me through the highs and lows of my life. For children growing up in such a wicked and carnal world, having a belief system built on sound doctrine is no less important than it was for all who have come before them. If they do not have parents committed to this vital training, it becomes even more important for our churches to do the work Jesus sacrificed for the church to do. The Church must win souls through God's Christ. I challenge churches to give these children a belief system that can withstand the persecution that we've been warned will come in the End Times. I am grateful for my relationship with the God of my belief system. I learned about and got to know the God of my belief system in church and in my home. To God be the glory!

My dear Muslim friend and co-worker, Zoubida Kettani and me

Ms. Myrtle Williams

Wimp nicknamed her Knuckles. He claimed that one Sunday when she was playing the introduction to a song for the choir to sing, he looked down at the organ and it looked as though she were playing the keys with her knuckles. The name stuck. We only used it in privacy and in close company. The youth of First Baptist Church NBC loved and respected our musician and would never dream of hurting her feelings.

Ms. Myrtle Williams was a servant-musician. She rehearsed every choir in the church, played for every choir performance and for every worship service at home and whenever the choirs were scheduled as guests in other places. She was present and accounted for, even when we were not. Her service to First Baptist NBC will no doubt ensure her a reward in Heaven. She was literally faithful until the day she died.

Ms. Williams taught me and others like me, nearly every Christian song I learned from the age of five to age nineteen. She was humble and never appeared to be concerned about being recognized although her service to the Christian people of First Baptist NBC was only exceeded by the service of our pastor. The service of no other member came close.

She always reminded me of Annie from the classic movie, *Imitation of Life*. She was a dark-skinned African American woman. She was robust. She wore a wig that had a page-boy cut. She earned her income as a maid and often times wore her work uniform to church on Wednesdays. She only wore dresses. On Sundays, she may have worn her Sunday-best outfit, but I have no memory of an opinion of how she dressed because she always wore a choir robe. She always dressed for service.

Sometimes Ms. Williams would bring secular music to choir rehearsal. After rehearsal was over, we would stand over her shoulder around the piano and sing songs like "Yesterday," "Moon River," and "Raindrops Keep Falling on My Head." We would look like teenagers gathered around the piano after Thanksgiving dinner at grandma's house. She would grin. She was surrounded by her children, having fun and everyone was glad to be there experiencing that moment. She was not going to let a "generation gap" separate her from her children. She had found a way to genuinely engage us into looking forward to our time together.

Ms. Williams's talents as a musician were limited. She was restricted to reading music. If the music was written in a key that was too high or too low for our voices, it was too bad. If you wanted to learn a song or sing a song for which she had no music or time to practice, she could not accompany you with music. With Ms. Williams, no music meant no music.

We discovered a new limitation to Ms. Williams's musician skills one evening when we were on program as a guest choir at a church that was known for having great choirs. We were prepared. We were wearing our new gold-colored choir robes with green ties, so we were dressed for success. We had rehearsed our most popular song. We had a plan. We were ready.

The choir that had sung prior to our getting into the choir stand had moved the crowd. The organist had skills and was just as much a feature as a soloist. The music from the organ added to the choir's presentation. Although the choir was intimidating, we rallied, maintained our confidence and took the stand. We had a plan that would make Ms. Williams's musical limitations be enough for the occasion. We would survive.

While we were waiting to hear the introduction to the song we had prepared to sing, strange musical chords filled the atmosphere. We were stunned and looked at each other in wonder about where those disruptive sounds could be coming from. I remember personally thinking that the chimes of the nearby Baylor University were projecting a great distance and would soon cease. Imagine our surprise when Ms. Williams spoke out and told us to "Come on," and motioned for us to sing.

She had played the song's introduction a couple of times, and we had missed it because we did not recognize it. The previous choir's musician had set the organ to make sounds that enhanced their performance. The combination of chords worked wonderfully for their contemporary sound, but they were death chords to our traditional sound. We had a plan to give our traditional sound, a contemporary twist, despite Ms. Williams's limitations, but we were not prepared for Ms. Williams's inability to know how to restore the organ keys to a traditional sound.

We sang that day. The music sounded like that of an organ grinder's. We were as humiliated as monkeys performing to the music of an organ-grinder. The congregation was as stunned as we. They sat politely, stared, and listened until we vacated the choir stand and the building. Rita, Nita, Cheryl, and I went home. Other choir members followed, and we debriefed the most humiliating experience we had ever suffered together as a choir.

We wanted a new musician. This was the final straw. This was the straw that broke the camel's back. We finally had the missing piece to the puzzle that would make Papa Hardee get us a better, more qualified and skillful musician. The music was horrible, and she was clueless. She sat on the organ, playing that "monkey music," singing and grinning like she was intentionally sabotaging our plan to impress the congregation despite her limited musical ability.

Surely Pastor Hardee will agree with us and get rid of her because she had embarrassed our beloved First Baptist Church NBC. We criticized, "She doesn't even know how to adjust the keys on an organ." That was the experience that caused all of us to refer to Ms. Williams as Knuckles, but again, never to her face or where she would ever know.

Needless to say, Ms. Williams continued being our musician. Papa Hardee understood what we did not. She was a faithful servant of God. No one could replace her deep commitment to service as the musician of our church, especially for the little amount of money she earned doing it. Ms. Williams was working out her soul's salvation with fear and trembling while full of joy, by providing music, so we could worship. I am so glad Papa Hardee was a wise shepherd.

Ms. Williams continued serving First Baptist Church NBC faithfully for many more years. She used her life to demonstrate what loyalty and commitment and dedication look like. She served as First Baptist's musician until she died. Legend has it, she was dressed for church when they found her dead on her bedroom floor. She had neither called nor shown up for duty by service time, so a couple of deacons had gone to her home to check on her. What a faithful servant! I am reminded of one of the many songs she taught us. The words are, "When He calls me, I will answer. I'll be somewhere listening for my name." Ms. Myrtle Williams heard her name and answered.

The Organist, Ms. Myrtle Williams

Ms. Myrtle

Let me know when Myrtle arrives.
I want to go and meet her at the Gate.
I do not want to wait
Ten thousand years for our paths to cross.
I want no lost time before
My eyes look upon the hands
Of a woman with such a faithful heart.
She will start eternity searching for a place to serve.
She will want to give God the glory He deserves
Right away.
Oh what a happy day when
She will hear the Master say to her
Servant, well done.
Welcome home.
Notify me when she comes.
I want to witness the surprise in her eyes.

Francene student-teaching at University High School in 1982

Life to Lyrics

I have lived more than five decades. Over three of those decades, I have been employed with the Waco Independent School District; twenty as a classroom teacher and fourteen as an administrator. I have worked with educating students from pre-K through the twelfth grade. What a journey my work experience has given me!

Robert Fulghum, a fellow Native Wacoan wrote the poem, *All I Really Need to Know I Learned in Kindergarten*. Its lyrics are powerful and true. The kindergartner who learns the lessons Fulghum's poem expounds will be better equipped to enjoy life as an adult. It is my belief that it is essential for five-year-olds to learn to live according to valuable character traits.

Proverbs 22:6 renders the same advice as Fulghum's this way, "Train up a child in the way he should go: and when he is old, he will not depart from it." Lack of training and maleficent training are as equally influential on the adult life of a kindergartner. For this reason, parents and educators must unite in our efforts to give our children, especially the most destitute among them, the skill sets they need to enjoy life as a citizen of the United States of America. They must be taught to appreciate the liberty they have as they pursue happiness within the confines of the laws of our land.

That is what my parents, public school educators and Christian educators gave me. My poems transform my life into lyrics in an effort to use my story to pay their gifts to me forward. Each poem tells a person's story or tells a lesson inspired by my encounter with a person. I am spending the closing years of my life refreshing and updating the sum total of the experiences that compose my life.

The older I get, the more valuable the experiences I had living at the corner of Lenox and Turner become. The tradition in Nairobi is to refer to your childhood home as Home Squared, "home twice over" (Obama 2004). I processed an understanding of myself and my life's experiences in the safety and comfort of 728 Lenox in Waco, Texas, Haliburton Home Squared. I pray that readers also find value in their own childhood memories and experiences.

"The eye is the window of the soul," according to Shakespeare and Leonardo DaVinci who are among other famous people credited with saying so. To believe this, one may also believe that with a careful search of another person's eyes, one should be able to determine that person's intent. Looking diligently into a person's eyes may reveal whether or not the person is a friend or foe, whether the person intends you harm or intends you good or bids you welcome or rejection.

If one can discover the heart of another by searching his/her eyes, then searching the eyes of another is paramount to survival and as such becomes a skill vitally important to be developed for accuracy. Long before I knew of "the window to the soul philosophy," I knew that there was something vitally important about looking into the eyes of others in order to discern their intent. Even as a little African American girl, I learned to depend upon my ability to read safety or harm in the eyes of others because experience had taught me that most of the time, I was right about what I was interpreting from searching the eyes of others.

Staring into the eyes of a white man or woman was once considered disrespectful and a dangerous thing for an African American person to do. While the eyes of the Negro were to bear witness to whether or not he/she were telling the truth by the experts who took pride in being able to tell the difference, a Negro had no reasonable expectation for the same opportunity to search the eyes of their white counterparts in search of the truth by the same technique.

There were dangerous white men who dared African Americans to look into the windows of their souls while in the same breath demanded to search for whatever ugliness they could uncover from the soul of a black man or woman in an exhaustive search. In America, where all men, all mankind were believed to be created equally, this search technique was not allowed to work both ways.

As an African American woman living in the twenty-first century, I have the privilege of freely using the skills I developed as a child to search the eyes of others in order to determine my comfort level with trusting the words coming out of their mouths. I also have the right to deflect the search into my own soul from someone seeking to discover the ugliness that may be subject to the beholder's judgment. I welcome others to the responsible behavior of searching my eyes for the truth, though it may seem to some a weak assessment tool. It challenges the irresponsible behavior of those who would still judge me according to the color of my skin.

In 2015, one of my sisters overheard two elderly white women talking at a nursing home facility. One said to the other, "You know it's a shame that black folk don't fear white people the way they used to." I doubt that the little old lady realized how she sounded. She probably had no intentions of being overheard. Had she made that statement within earshot of a less compassionate African American individual than my sister, she might have had an experience she would have regretted having. The little old white lady had elevated her social skills to tolerate integration, but she seemed to be longing for a day when simply the color of her skin was an advantage that made her a threat and/or warning to African Americans.

I am so grateful that there are so many color-blind, white Americans in this day and time. I have had the pleasure of working with many of them for more than three decades. They are genuinely so non-tolerant of racist behavior that they have insulated their worlds against racist comments and behaviors. Living in a silo such as this, however, causes some to believe that racism no longer exists or is no longer a viable threat to African Americans. This could not be further from the truth.

Most African Americans I know stay on guard against racism. In fact, I personally believe that there is an increase in racism in America that requires us to sound an alarm. I am becoming more and more challenged in my ability to interpret the meaning of a negative encounter I may have with a white person. I have begun to struggle with determining whether the conflict is the result of that white person's way of mistreating everyone or whether the white person is mistreating me because I am black. I have felt welcomed in the company of varying races of people since I was five years old. I believed we were making progress with integrating our country to a level of comfort for nearly every American. I am so concerned about the grounds we have begun losing. African Americans will be the biggest loser in this age of racial regression. It saddens me.

Varying races must not stop trying to live and function compassionately and peacefully among each other. We must all commit to lifestyles that exemplify noble character. We must value these lifestyles deeply enough to assure their survival from generation to generation. We should all strive to be great Americans. More and more, younger African Americans have begun to fear that using noble characteristics when engaging others makes them vulnerable and weak. African Americans are survivors, and we operate on the premise "Only the strong survive." We have to reconcile the notion that African Americans can be both noble and strong in our dealings with our fellow man.

When you are out shopping late, you may recall hearing an announcement that sounds something like this, "It's almost closing time. Please make your final selections and proceed to the checkout." When you hear that announcement, you know that it is time for you to make up your mind about your shopping selections. You have to decide whether or not you are going to put something back. You have to decide if you are going to return to an area to get something that you had decided to go ahead and purchase. Sometimes you have to go back by a department and pick up something that you told yourself you would get on the way out. When you hear that announcement, you know that you only have a limited amount of time left to shop, and you must make your final purchasing decisions in a hurry.

It's almost closing time in life for most of us in our middle ages. We likely have more years behind us than we have ahead of us. We are in a stage in our lives that forces us to come face-to-face with thoughts of death and dying nearly every day. The older we are, the more we think about it. We also think more about our own deaths as relatives, friends, and classmates die. Like shopping, it is time for us to make our final selections in life as we proceed toward the checkout.

We have entered those years, where we reflect, or should be reflecting, on our past. We reflect on the best of our experiences and the worst of our experiences. We reflect upon what we consider our best decisions and on what we consider our worst decisions. We reflect with regrets upon the choices of people we attached to our lives, as well as reflect with regrets on the people we did not attach to our lives. It is almost closing time in our lives.

I am so grateful for the many decades that God has been good to my family and me. When we are together, we sometimes reflect on the various experiences we have shared throughout these years. Our family's stories are similar to the stories of many other families: white, black, and brown. We all have some common experiences and stories in our lives.

Some have the pride of becoming a bride or a groom in common. Others share the joy of becoming a mother, a father, a grandmother, a grandfather in common. Many of us know the experience of falling in love with Jesus being the best thing we've ever, ever done. We've bought homes, favorite cars, high-fashioned clothing, shoes, and handbags. We've climbed the career ladders on our jobs, and some have even retired. We've had favorite movies in common, favorite songs (religious and secular).

We remember where we were in 2001 when Al-Qaeda attacked our country on 9/11. We remember how we felt when we got the news that Michael Jackson was dead and that Whitney Houston was gone. We can recall where we were when OJ was found "not guilty." African Americans remember the disappointment we felt when we saw that there was no plan in place to rescue the black people in New Orleans who had survived Hurricane Katrina and the pride we felt in November 2008 when America elected Barack Obama the first black President of the United States.

We were living our lives in different cities, but we yet had similar emotional experiences. We have survived so much in our lives. We used the tools our parents gave us in our homes. We used the tools our teachers gave us in our schools. We used the tools the preachers gave us in our churches. We survived using our tools to protect our-selves from bullies, racism, and ignorance on our jobs, in the places where we do business, and against the discriminative laws and prac-tices of those in authoritative positions.

Our forefathers and foremothers gave us survival tools; they gave us shortcuts to success. They taught us "escape routes" to life's pitfalls. They made sacrifices for us, so we could not only survive, but also be successful. They prepared us, so we could survive past the closing times in their lives.

Now, for us, it's almost closing time in our lives, and our African American children are in trouble. They face challenges we never had to face and sadly, more of them are less prepared than we ever were. As a people, we have provided our children more material possessions than our parents could provide us, even with their sacrifices, but as a people, we have left our children far less prepared to endure life's hardships than the hardships for which our parents, grandparents, and great-grandparents prepared us.

Some of our children are willing to take a life in exchange for the newest name brand athletic shoe. Some will kill because they are rejected by someone they had hoped to marry. College professors are murdered because of assigning a disappointing grade. Supervisors and employers have been killed because they fired an employee. Young men take revenge for losing a fight by taking the life of the one who embarrassed them. Some of our children behave as though they don't know it is wrong for them to kill people when they don't get their way. Killing someone has now become our children's solu-tion to their problems. It is almost closing time in our lives, and our children are in trouble.

Before we close our eyes, we need to do whatever we can to ensure that if in the year 2525 man is still alive, that there are African American men thriving equally among them. We need to have a strong number of healthy, successful African American men and women among the healthy, successful white American men and women. We want our African American descendants to be noble, patriotic, and full of integrity. Some of us even want them to have deep spiritual conviction. African Americans with violent, criminal behaviors put us all in danger. In our communities, we must teach against embracing a life of violence. We must also teach those outside our communities that we have an equal right to the pursuit of happiness in this country we share without being judged by different standards only because the color of our skin is different. We need to leave our young, African American children as ready as we possibly can leave them to survive the challenges in their future whenever the closing time in life comes for us. Failure is not an option.

We fear what we don't understand. It is human nature as well as animal nature. We are even more fearful of people and things we cannot control. White people in the United States of America are becoming increasingly more fearful of African Americans. Unfortunately, all fears are not without merit. Intentional care must be given to assure that fearing African Americans does not retard the social, racial and civil progress in our country.

Many of us are more alike than we are different. We worship the same God identified in The Holy Bible. We love and care for our family members. We take pride in our heritage. We are proud to be Americans, and we enjoy our rights as citizens. We expect to have our rights to life, liberty and the pursuit of happiness protected. We make mistakes. We say and do things that we later regret. We say and do things that people may judge as bad. That does not make us bad people. We are each, "a work in progress," and in need of understanding from others.

Take time to get to know one African American's story up close. Compare and contrast my experiences to your own. We are the sum total of the choices we allow to influence us. Read my story. Make an effort to understand me, especially if it is your initial effort to understand any African American. White people have nothing to fear from me nor from most African Americans. We do not have to be controlled before we are looked upon without fear. White people who cannot be controlled are more often treated with respect than not. They are likely not looked upon with fear.

African Americans should be able to raise our voices and express our anger as do white Americans without being judged as someone who is out of control and someone to be feared. Don't assume that because I am an African American that I love this country less than a patriotic white American. I am no more embarrassed that my ancestors arrived to this country as slaves than white people are embarrassed that their ancestors hypocritically violated the laws of this country by enslaving Africans.

Even after African Americans were set free in 1865, the laws in our country did not provide them adequate protection for their rights as citizens. In fact, the laws protected from consequences those who violated the rights of African Americans. Until the Civil Rights Movement of the 1950s, 1960s and 1970s and the rise in the leadership of Dr. Martin Luther King Jr., African Americans were treated by most white Americans as second class citizens. The aforementioned Civil Rights Movement changed that. As a result, Presidential candidate, Robert F. Kennedy accurately predicted in 1968 that America could elect an African American as President of the United States in forty years. In November 2008, Barak Hussein Obama became our forty-forth President.

When I reflect on how white Americans have treated African Americans in my country, I see three major trends. The first trend spans over three hundred years in time. (The first slaves arrived here in 1619.) This trend includes the stages of slavery up to the years that led to the sweeping changes acquired as a result of the Civil Rights Movement. In 1712, Willie Lynch addressed a group of American slave owners. He guaranteed them three hundred years of being able to control their slaves if the owners implemented his methods of programming the slaves socially, emotionally and psychologically. Lynch's methods still impact African Americans' lives even today. I refer to this trend as the period when African Americans were rejected.

I refer to the second trend as the period when African Americans were protected. After the end of slavery, the greatest achievements in the human and civil rights of African Americans occurred during The Civil Rights Movement between the 1950s and 1970s. Affirmative Action was designed and implemented in an effort to systemically fast-track African Americans' access to and assimilation into American society's social and economic channels of success. Affirmative Action forced government agencies and government funded institutions to provide guaranteed economic opportunities for African Americans. It became wildly unpopular. Critics of Affirmative Action successfully marketed its destruction by referring to it as a quota system.

By the time the statute of limitations had run out on Affirmative Action, the noble concept of its original purpose was dead on arrival. The period of protecting African Americans by guaranteeing us a seat at the tables of economic empowerment in a variety of arenas and venues came to an end and ushered in the present trend.

I call the present trend of how some white Americans have treated African Americans in the USA the period of neglect. During the period of the first trend, African Americans were rejected from gaining access to economic opportunities. The trend that followed protected African Americans and guaranteed us access to the opportunities we as a people had previously been denied. This present period of neglect neither rejects nor protects African Americans' access to economic empowerment. Many white Americans with power do not seem to care either way what happens to African Americans. As a people in general, African Americans have been left on our own to navigate systems that were originally designed to keep us out. Many white Americans have grown comfortable with the idea that they have a right to isolate themselves as far away from undesirable people as possible. Unfortunately, too many of them categorize nearly all African Americans as undesirable simply because of the color of our skin.

We live in a world where entire neighborhoods are in gated communities and protected by private security companies. Who can afford this, and who cannot? It is only a matter of time before vouchers will redirect public tax dollars away from public education in order to finance education in private institutions. Private educational institutions have the right to accept or reject their students. Who will be accepted, and who will be rejected in these institutions?

If African Americans are not intentionally welcomed to the tables of economic opportunities by design, we will be left further and further behind as white Americans make exponential gains. If white Americans continue to widen the gap in their interactions with African Americans, their fear of African Americans will grow. As their fear of African Americans grows, so will their desire to increase the gap in their interactions with us. Many white Americans are finding little to no value in retaining relationships with African Americans. This line of thought is not only a mistake, but it is also a dangerous one.

African Americans are the canaries of American society. If this is the most significant role white Americans can find for reasons to value African Americans, it is enough to assure our survival in a world of economic progress. At best, assuring the survival and access to economic progress for African Americans is a humanitarian responsibility.

Natural gas has no odor. A repugnant scent is added to gas in order to make the human nose aware of its deadly presence. During the early years of mining, the release of poisonous gases into the environment would overpower miners, render them unconscious and result in death. Because the gas is naturally odorless, there was no way to detect its presence before it was too late for the miners.

Miners used canaries to solve this fatal threat. Caged canaries would be carried into the mines and stand guard while the miners focused on their work. Should deadly gas be released into the environment, the canaries would die long before the miners were in danger. The miners simply had to monitor the canaries to determine their level of danger. The poison affected the canaries first.

I call on white American citizens who could not care less about African Americans to save America's social canaries. Interests in the African American experience is becoming more and more appealing to the younger white Americans. They want to experience our music, our dance moves, and vices identified as African Americans' vices.

There are so many experiences to be explored about the African American culture. Older white Americans will need to increase their understanding of African Americans in order to be able to understand their children and grandchildren's attraction to the culture. They will be wise to take an interest in African Americans since African Americans have their children and grandchildren's interests. Save the canaries; save the children/grandchildren. One will discover that white Americans and African Americans have more in common than we have differences. There is nothing to fear.

Benjamin Franklin advised, "God helps those who help themselves." Serious, heartbreaking, dysfunctional behaviors are occurring in today's African American communities. Unfortunately, we are becoming less shocked by these behaviors being displayed among the people where we live. Although it is essential for white Americans to shoulder some responsibilities for relieving the struggles transpiring in our African American communities, the greatest responsibilities must be shouldered by the African American people ourselves. If we accept that the God who loves us expects us to help ourselves, how much more should we accept that white Americans also expect us to help ourselves and not expect them to do all the work necessary for improving our communities? Each of us must prepare ourselves in an academic discipline or in an area of service that will give us skills that others can value. African Americans must take action to help ourselves.

We need the cooperation of white Americans, but we, more importantly, need to take responsibility for the preservation of our own culture and for carving out a niche for ourselves in the future of American progress and success. It is not helpful for white Americans to live their lives treating African Americans as if white skin automatically makes them better than and superior to people blessed to be born with black skin. Neither is it helpful for those of us blessed to be born with black skin to behave in ways that keeps those who were blessed to be born in white skin from realizing that the color of our skin does not determine our value. African American brothers and sisters, behave as though you understand your value yourself. Act like a great American.

Fight

I wish I could truthfully say that I have never had to fight for anything, but I cannot. The training I received in my home, in my school, and in my church all taught me that it was wrong to fight. We should not hurt others. However, literally, as well as figuratively, I know what it means to fight for everything I value except food. Poor people, even poor black people, in America can get food when they can't get anything else. I have never been hungry due to someone's inability to provide food. On the other hand, fighting for rights has been a lifelong daily battle. I know what it means to fight for my right to property, to due process, to an opportunity, to prove I am capable. I have fought for money, for love, for objects and symbols. I have fought for friends, for family, for myself, for respect, for pride, for vengeance.

I have fought verbal wars in the kitchen, as well as in the classroom for my country because even when it appears that my country is fighting against me, I still believe that this is the greatest country ever known to man. This country is beautiful, and it harbors the grace of God. It is crowned with greatness and with goodness from sea to shining sea. Unfortunately, I learned firsthand as a child the struggle of African American people in my beloved country.

In 1968, Daddy and I were shopping in a variety store called Gibsons in Waco, Texas. I remember thinking, "It sure is late to be shopping," because it was already dark outside. Connecting outside darkness with a late hour of the day was probably due to my perception as an eight-year-old child. Another African American man greeted my father. Soon after, my father's words and tone disturbed me deeply. He set down the basket of items on the aisle floor, and said to me with such deep sadness, "Let's go. I don't even want to shop anymore."

I didn't recognize the man's name, but I could tell by Dad's reaction that the news that the man had been shot and killed had upset him tremendously. I didn't recognize the man's name as one of Dad's friends or cousin or some other relative whose names were familiar to me. I only knew that the man who had been shot and killed was someone important to my dad, someone he loved.

That night, I learned the definition of the word "assassination." It was April 4, 1968, the night James Earl Ray Jr. murdered Dr. Martin Luther King Jr. in Memphis, Tennessee. The beautiful and spacious skies of America had suddenly turned to low-hanging dark clouds of gray. I felt threatened by the news although I could not understand why. Being born African American in a 1950s America, I automatically inherited my fight for racial equality.

Two months later, the intensity of my fears increased when I watched my dad deal with the news of Robert F. Kennedy's assassination. R. F. K.'s murder made everyone relive the assassination of his brother, President of the United States John F. Kennedy, as well as Dr. King's.

I did not know what to think about my future in America. I pledged my allegiance. I memorized the words and sang, "My country tis' of thee, sweet land of liberty." But the Sunday school teacher and others at church, including my pastor (whom I believed spoke nothing but the truth) all talked about the end of the world. Many other respected adults in my daily life were discussing world events and asking some form of the question, "What is this world coming to?"

Adding to my alarm and fears, the radio, a primary source of reliable news, everyday played Skeeter Davis's song, "The End of the World," several times a day. America was at war against North Vietnam. For me, the right to live meant the need to fight. Though I had no understanding about the value of rights, especially as an American, I understood the connection between fighting and surviving. African Americans, or at that time Negroes, were fighting to survive in America.

I was a Negro, so for me, the fight was for my survival. For me, the Negroes' fight in America was for the survival of all the Negroes in my home, in the Haliburton Family, in the Vonner Family, at Dripping Springs Elementary School, at First Baptist Church, NBC and all my neighbors in Carver Park Addition.

I suspect that most white children growing up in America during the tumultuous fifties, sixties, and seventies did not give much thought to fighting and surviving as Negro children did. Talk of racial injustice in America was in our homes, in our schools, in our churches, and at our social gatherings throughout Waco, Texas. The white children with whom I came in contact in Waco appeared to be enjoying life just like the white children I saw on television.

The lives of white boys in Waco looked like Wally and Beaver's lives from the show *Leave It to Beaver*, like Dennis's from *Dennis the Menace*, like Little Ricky's from *I Love Lucy*, like Little Richie from *The Dick Van Dyke Show*, and like Opie's from *The Andy Griffith Show*. The little white girls' worries seemed similar to Patti's and Cathy's from the *Patti Duke Show*, similar to Billie Jo and Bobbie Jo and Betty Jo's problems from *Petticoat Junction*, and Kitty's from *Father Knows Best* and Marsha, Jan, and Cindy Brady's problems from "The Brady Bunch."

I recall three major annual parades in downtown Waco: the Baylor University Homecoming Parade, the Heart of Texas Fair and Rodeo Parade and the Christmas Parade. The Baylor Parades always had various floats decorated in green and gold. I loved all the sparkling colors, the excitement from the bands and twirlers. The HOT Fair and Rodeo Parade was always heavily decorated in red, white and blue. It was exciting to me because of all of the horses. The Christmas Parade was my favorite for obvious reasons. Christmas meant gifts, special foods and family, and the Christmas Parade decorated in shiny Christmas colors, signaled the season for gifts and toys. Everybody in every parade, every year was either a white man, white woman, white boy, or white girl.

While my mind as a child was focused on learning from my African American parents, teachers, and other African American role models how to survive as a Negro in America, I believed white girls

133

in Waco were enjoying themselves every day the way white girls on television and those I saw in the parades were enjoying themselves.

I did not know the significance of Rosa Parks nor Emmett Till on the history of the United States during the tumultuous years of the Civil Rights Movement. I could not even remember their names, but as a child growing up in the southern state of Texas, I knew their stories. I referenced Rosa Parks as, "the lady who wouldn't give up her seat on the bus," whenever I spoke of her or thought of her. When speaking or thinking of Emmett Till, I knew him as, "the boy who whistled at a white woman."

As a little black girl growing up in Texas, I was mindful of the seemingly harmless behaviors that could get black people arrested or brutally killed, even children. Television provided an indelible vision of the hatred some whites had for people of color. I watched *To Kill a Mockingbird* year after year. My heart raced with fear while sitting in the safe comfort of my home watching the innocent Negro character, Tom Robinson, on the television screen endure the racial prejudice and hate-filled experiences that would lead to his death. Whenever I thought of "the lady" and "the little boy," I knew that these experiences were not limited to television. They were happening to people: good people, black people like me.

I worried about the women in my neighborhood who caught the bus to and from work. Five or six women could be seen walking to the bus stop wearing their white uniforms, headed to work as maids in other parts of town. Sometimes Mrs. Carter would wear her gray uniform. Often times, the white people for whom she worked would drive her home long after all the other ladies had gotten home on the bus.

I thought Mrs. Carter was a special maid like Hazel from the television show bearing the same name. Mrs. Carter was quiet and kept to herself. She walked to the bus stop alone. She used her beautiful umbrella to shield her from the sun's heat. She kept her hair, neatly tucked under a thin hairnet. She was a dark-skinned woman who reminded me of Juanita Moore who played the maid, Annie Johnson and mother to the character Sarah Jane in the movie, *Imitation of Life*. Seeing Mrs. Carter was a daily reminder of how sad it was for such good, kind people to have the misfortune of being black. Even your children may not love you until it is too late, the way it happened to Sarah Jane in the movie. Mrs. Carter had no children, so no worries there. I just hoped that she and all the other women who rode the buses daily knew that if a white man wanted her seat, she should just get up and give it to him.

I worried most about Daddy. Daddy was always on the go. For decades he worked from midnight to eight o'clock in the mornings at the local tire and rubber plant. He did most of his sleeping from 9:00 AM to 3:00 PM while we were at school. If he had church or some other civil service or community activity, he would get dressed in a starched white shirt, suit, and tie. The whole house would be filled with Daddy's aromas: aftershave and Right Guard deodorant. We knew Daddy was getting dressed, and he was going somewhere that we did not have to go, like church.

From the time Dad lathered and prepared his face for a shave until the time he put on his polished shoes, he would be singing and whistling. Daddy loved to do both, and he was good at both. There was beauty and bravado in Daddy's whistling. It was powerful and strong like I remember him to have been. His whistling wasn't brazen, brash, or intrusive. It was Daddy's musical instrument. Daddy loved to whistle, and he was good at it. Daddy spent a lot of time around white people when he went to meetings. I worried about him whistling around them and having his whistling mistaken as whistling at a white woman. I saw *To Kill a Mockingbird*. I knew that mistakes could get good innocent men killed, and whistling at a white woman got Emmett Till killed. I worried about Daddy.

My family members were members of First Baptist Church NBC, not to be confused with the white First Baptist Church two streets over and less than two miles south of our location. Our pastor was the late, great Dr. L. F. Hardee. That is Leon Fernandez Hardee. Our pastor's wife was the late, also great, Mrs. Johnnie Dee Waters-Hardee. The children and youth in the church affectionately called them Mama and Papa Hardee. Two of the finest Christians who ever slipped on a pair of shoes.

Mama and Papa Hardee were pillars of the African American community. They possessed all the major characteristics that impressed black people in those days except one. They had money. They were educated. They had the community's respect. He was dashingly handsome, and she was beautiful. He had "good" wavy hair that lay across his head, and she had skin complexion that would allow her to pass for white like Sarah Jane in the movie, *Imitation of Life*. Mama and Papa Hardee appeared to have everything black people valued in those days except biological children.

The Haliburton Family was the largest active family in the church. There were eight of us: two parents and six children. The Hicks Family had six children, but Mr. Hicks did not attend church. The Miller Family had six children, but their attendance was inconsistent. When the Haynes Family walked into our church for the first time, we saw that The Haliburton Family was licked. We were licked two ways. The Haliburtons had a set of twins, a distinguishing feature. The Haynes Family entered the sanctuary, and we started counting. There were six of them, and three of the girls were triplets. They were first cousins to The Browns who had joined our church with a family of five children. (In time, they added two children.)

This made the Brown Family the official, undisputed champions of seven. That is if you don't count Christi Hicks who was born five or six years later. Other circumstances that skewed the loving competition of number of members in a family included: Mom and Daddy divorced, and the Millers divorced. Naval Lt. Phillip Brown was killed in a car wreck. I remember those years as troubling times for all, but worse for some.

Regardless to family sizes, no other families could boast of having four active children in Sunday school, in the choirs, in Baptist Training Union every Sunday and at choir rehearsals and Youth Meeting every Wednesday like Rita, Nita, Francene, and Cheryl Haliburton were. Other families had one or two consistently present children. (Thank God for them.) Besides family gatherings and school activities, church activities consumed our social calendar for a decade. Mama and Papa Hardee made First Baptist Church NBC members a family, and the family bond among the children of First Baptist lasts to this day.

In 1963, four little black girls were killed when four men from a white supremacist group set off a bomb at the Sixteenth Street Baptist Church in Birmingham, Alabama. Twenty-two others were injured. People in our community still talked about the tragedies of The Civil Rights Movement cautiously five, six and ten years later. It was the seventies, but we were still in the struggle. It could be deadly to be black and fighting for your "rights." Why did whites hate us so much? They were willing to bomb our churches, to kill the children who went to Sunday school? Rita, Nita, Cheryl, and I went to Sunday school, and we were black.

The Sixteenth Street Baptist Church in Birmingham was the place of worship for a large black congregation. Whenever the black community needed a venue large enough to accommodate an event of common interest, the Sixteenth Street Baptist Church was used. The church hosted meetings in preparation for fighting for the civil rights of the African Americans in their community.

We lived across the street from the Carver Park Baptist Church. The church was in the heart of our East Waco community known as Carver Park. When the fight for civil rights exploded in our community, it was over integrating schools. The year was 1970. The African American high school students from our community had staged an impromptu protest. They had been welcomed by Pastor Robert L. Booker to gather during school hours at the Carver Park Baptist Church. That night, once the working parents and citizens of the community were available, they met at the church to decide what would be done to support their children.

There were so many people and so many cars parked for blocks. Some in the community lived close enough to walk to the meeting. Men and women stood on the outside, listening through opened windows to the discussions being held inside. I was ten, nearly eleven. I wondered why the meeting had not been held at a larger church like First Baptist NBC.

First Baptist Church NBC. was often used to host church gatherings that involved a multitude of churches and pastors. I'd seen the success of this venue choice enough times to know that the crowd gathered at Carver Park Baptist Church that night should have made arrangements with Papa Hardee to meet at First Baptist NBC. Papa Hardee was cautious in his involvement and participation in the civil rights movement that had come to Waco, to the people of Carver Park. My fears told a ten-year-old me that Papa Hardee was probably right.

The Sixteenth Street Baptist Church had been targeted because the congregation and pastor had allowed their church to be used as a meeting place in the fight for civil rights in Birmingham. Members of the KKK bombed the church as a consequence. Fourteen-year-olds Addie Mae Collins, Cynthia Wesley, Carole Robertson, and eleven-year-old Carol Denise McNair went to Sunday school on September 15, 1963, and lost their lives because they were black.

Papa Hardee was right. I was already worried. There were whites who hated blacks. Whites who were willing to bomb churches and willing to kill little girls who attended Sunday school actually existed. They were not found only on television. I was just beginning to have fewer fears about how negatively I believed most white people felt about black people. The few weeks that we had been attending integrated schools had caused me to drop my guard. The events that ushered the Civil Rights Movement into the Carver Park Community in 1970 also refreshed my fears from past memories.

It was 1968, and Daddy wanted to be the county commissioner of Precinct 3. Suddenly, Daddy was more involved in politics than ever before, and so was I. He hit the campaign trail, and I tagged along. I was eight years old, with little understanding about all of the highs and lows of the environments I was entering, going wherever Daddy went. On the way to an event, he talked; I listened and pretended to understand. Upon leaving an event, he talked; I listened and pretended to understand.

It was 1968. I was in the third grade. My teacher was a popular busybody. My parents were separated, pending a nasty public divorce. The whole country was depressed because some guy named Billie Joe McAlister had jumped off the Tallahatchie Bridge. The African American communities throughout the United States were mourning the losses of Abraham, Martin and John. I had begun to suffer with seizures, and the Brazos River had claimed the life of my eight-year-old second-cousin, Ronald Earl White. Daddy was running for public office.

I didn't know their names, but I knew that two good white men and a black man had been murdered in Mississippi for trying to register black people to vote. I believed Mississippi to be a dangerous place for poor black people who could not afford to get out. I believed the white people of Mississippi hated the black people there. I remembered Daddy and Papa Hardee driving to Mississippi with a station wagon full of clothes and food. The people there had suffered great losses as a result of a tornado.

The African American community in Waco had not forgotten their own experience with a devastating tornado in 1953 and were eager to send supplies to the affected Mississippi community. Daddy and Papa Hardee traveled together in our car to represent First Baptist Church NBC's contribution to that effort from the Waco, Texas, community. I was proud of my dad. People counted on him, even people in Mississippi was my thought.

Daddy had safely returned from Mississippi years earlier. Even as young as I was, I knew Mississippi to be a dangerous place for black people. James Chaney, Andrew Goodman, and Michael Schuwerner had been killed in Mississippi for trying to register black people to vote. Now Daddy was running for county commissioner, and he was on the campaign trail which included his duty to get people to register to vote. My daddy was brave, but I was scared. Evil white men had no problem killing little black girls, especially if they are somewhere trying to register people to vote.

We lived in McLennan County. Daddy was reared in the Gerald Community. Dad was no stranger to the people of West, Abbott, Gholson, and Elm Mott, neighboring communities of Gerald. He knew all of the dark, back roads of each of the communities. He talked to people who lived in these communities, people who would ask him to go by and examine the conditions of particular roads and bridges they crossed daily. They wanted to vote for a commissioner who would do something about the problems they faced, even if he were a black man.

Dad and I looked at some bridges and crossed them. We looked at others and backed out until we could find place to turn the car around. We drove down roads so narrow that the thick greenery growing on the roadside scraped against my side of the car. Sometimes Daddy would even say, "I hope I'm not scratching up my car."

Dad and I visited homes. We visited businesses. We walked past the stench of hog pens. We attended events such as the one where I had an opportunity to meet State Representative Lane Denton and his wife, Betty who later also became the representative of her husband's district. (She would years later become my seventh-grade English teacher before assuming her husband's seat.) I met attorneys. I met professors and college students. I met elderly adults who could not read.

I remember that Dad met with people who walked or caught a ride everywhere they went. He met with people who drove the latest model cars every time the local dealership told them it was time to upgrade. I met Governor of Texas John Connally as a result of my political adventures with Daddy. Somewhere lost in time and carelessness is my program of an event I attended and got Governor Connally's autograph. (He was shot and had survived the attack of the Presidential assassin, Lee Harvey Oswald years earlier.)

I was cautious in remembering that not all white people were evil. Neither were all white people good. The ones Daddy trusted were all right for me to trust too. White men, guns, and death all seemed to go together for me. I felt safe whenever I was with Dad, but I must admit, I had a few uncomfortable moments when I was afraid.

On one particular occasion, Dad and I had been out. It had grown dark, and the dark roads of the "countryside" were especially scary to me. I was relieved when a little convenience store seemed to pop up out of nowhere, and Dad pulled in. I was treated to a soda while Dad and the white men in the store chatted. I heard bits and pieces of their conversation, but I was not paying close attention. One of the white men got my attention when he asked if I wanted to see the hide of a boa constrictor he had killed. The man had come upon the snake soon after the snake had swallowed a hog.

I was fascinated by the story and the beautiful colors in the snake skin. Guns, white men, and death. I was ready to go. I had school the next day, and it was getting late. It was too close to my bedtime for me to be looking at the skin of a snake that had been killed by a white man with a gun. I did not need to risk having a nightmare. I was just learning to sleep in a bed, in a room by myself.

Mom and Dad were officially separated. Bruce, Dad, and I had moved into the apartment complex down the street from our family home on Lenox. Bruce and Dad shared a room in the two-bedroom apartment, and I had a room of my own. I had shared a bed with my oldest sister, Judy for as long as I could remember. Rita, Nita, Judy, and I shared a room in our home. We called it "The Girls' Room." Suddenly, I found myself spending more and more time alone and lonely. I was always glad to hear the key turn in the lock, even if entering the apartment was my brother, Bruce whom I would today call a bully.

Bruce and Judy were our oldest siblings. She was older. She was bossy, and she was "mean." Bruce was the only male sibling with five sisters. Rita, Nita, Cheryl, and I had no problem giving him the respect he felt he was entitled as a male of the fifties and sixties. After all, he was older than we were. Judy, on the other hand, was older than he. They battled over who had more power, the oldest child or the oldest and only son. Most times brawn won over beauty. Being Dad's only son wielded a lot of power.

Dad kept Bruce active in sports, school events, YMCA, and scouts to keep him from being bored around the house with five female siblings. Bruce was a typical boy in that he delighted in creating ways to agitate girls, especially sisters. Bruce was a bully. If Mom and Dad weren't home to stop him, Bruce's appetite for rough-housing was never satisfied until someone was in tears. That someone was usually me. I was either fighting my own battles with Bruce or the battles of Rita, Nita, or Cheryl.

Judy's battles with Bruce were Judy's to fight. First of all, she had a better chance of standing up to him because they were more closely matched in size and age. Secondly, if Bruce wasn't picking on one of the four of us, Judy was. Thirdly, I felt I always won whenever Bruce and Judy fought because they were both going to get hurt before it was over. I didn't particularly care who won the fight between the two of them.

In the summer months, when school was out, Judy would be in charge while our parents worked. She would make Cheryl and me go outside to play. She would make the twins clean the house while she read a book. (Judy and Rita loved to read.) Once Judy was satisfied with the results of Rita and Nita's housekeeping chores, she would put them outside with Cheryl and me. She wanted the house to stay clean for whenever my parents came home.

We had screen doors. We would knock and wait for Judy to answer. We could see her approaching the door aggravated. We knew how to cup our little hands to shield our eyes, so we could see inside the house. There were only two good reasons to knock on that door: water or restroom.

Judy was the oldest, so my parents had given her a little authority over the other girls. She was even allowed to spank us sometimes. One particular time that comes to mind may have been the last spanking I received from Judy. She was angry at me for bothering something that belonged to her. I think she was trying to spank me with a shoe. I felt I was ready to put a stop to this nonsense of getting a spanking from my sister, so I fought back. I decided to knock her glasses off her face. When she loosened her grip on me in order to pick them up from the floor, I tried to step on them and smash them. She wore my behind out before Daddy finally came to my rescue.

I lost sympathetic points with him once he found out that I had tried to break Judy's glasses. I sat on his lap in his favorite chair in the living room while he lectured me about what I had done wrong. He lectured; I listened and pretended to understand. If I didn't learn anything else, I learned that glasses cost money. I don't know which helped more to teach me a lesson that day, the spanking or the lecture. Trouble gets big fast if you do something wrong that costs money to replace. The good news is that that was the day that Judy stopped trying to spank me.

I would fight back. All my siblings knew that. Bruce took plea-sure in it. He knew what to say or what to do to get me stirred up enough to fight. He liked to put his hand on my head and hold me back at his arm's length. I would swing and kick at him hopelessly.

My last battle with Bruce occurred in the apartment we shared with Daddy. I was having a good time because Cheryl was spending the night with me. We were alone and playing with a wooden, puzzle map of the United States. Bruce came in and quickly changed my excitement to great sorrow. I knew there was going to be trouble. Even when a little girl can't explain it, prove it, or share evidence of it, she can experience enough trouble to be able to predict it on the horizon.

Sometimes Bruce would come home to the apartment, and he would sit and watch television with me. We would laugh and enjoy the programs until bed time. Other times, he would come in and turn the television away from something I would be watching. There was no use fighting with him at those times.

He would do other things to upset me as well. If I got out of my seat in front of the television to get a snack, go to the restroom, or to answer the phone, he would take my seat. He would stretch prostrate across the couch, so I could not sit down.

I had no idea that this fight between Bruce and me would be our last fight. I only knew that I had had enough of this bully. He was interfering with my time with Cheryl. I had looked forward to her coming to play. I was always alone in that apartment, and I had been accustomed to playing among a house full of sisters and espe-cially with Cheryl every day of my life until this separation happened to my family. This bully had to go away, so I could get back to my evening of pleasure.

The puzzle had a wooden base that cradled the pieces as you put the states of the United States in place. Bruce took the pieces out of the base and started showing Cheryl that the puzzle could be put together without the base. The bully had dismantled my puzzle and was entertaining my guest. To add insult to the injury, he was block-ing me and bumping me around with his butt, so I could neither see nor touch the puzzle pieces.

There were three major movements in this last battle between Bruce and me. Bruce was bent over with his butt raised in the air, a big beautiful clear target. I was holding the puzzle's wooden base in my hands, a big beautiful weapon. It seemed like a great idea, so I executed the plan in my head. Step 1, I swung the base back as far as I could. Step 2, I hit his butt as hard as I could with that wooden board. Step 3, Bruce turned and slapped me (I think as hard as he could). I don't remember any other activities about that evening. I do remember that that was the end of not only that battle, but also all battles with Bruce.

It was 1968. Daddy wanted to be the county commissioner of Precinct 3, and Mama wanted a divorce. I was in the third grade. I thought as a child. I spoke as a child. My understanding was that of a child. As an eight-year-old child, I already understood a great deal about lessons necessary to learn in life, sooner than I should have needed to learn them.

One Friday night, not only had Cheryl come to the apartment to spend the night, but the twins had also come. I was so happy to have them all over. Dad and I had picked the girls up after school as planned, so we could spend as much time together as possible. It felt like a big slumber party, among best friends. While we were all having a great time, Bruce included, something terrible was happening on Lenox.

Mr. Horace Coffee was married to Beatrice. They were our next door neighbors on Lenox until the day each died. They were father and mother figures to my parents. Mr. Coffee was Daddy's friend, and Mrs. Coffee was Mama's. My parents' divorce forced them to choose whose friend to be. They chose Mama. Daddy never got over his last encounter with Mr. Coffee. He would speak about it decades later and talk about it like it happened yesterday.

Mr. Coffee had worked for the railroad. He had been injured on the job and was unable to walk. He got around in a wheelchair. His transportation around town was an enclosed scooter for years. He eventually purchased a car that was outfitted for him to manage the gas and brake paddles with his hands.

Daddy and Mr. Coffee would take breaks from working and visit in the yard. Daddy would be mowing the grass, trimming the edges or clipping the hedges, and Mr. Coffee would pull up on his scooter and visit briefly. Mr. Coffee had a workshop behind his house. Sometimes Daddy would catch him in his workshop and spend time with him there.

My parents always demonstrated care and concern for their elders. Mr. Coffee had a son from a previous marriage about my dad's age. The son lived in New York. Mr. Coffee knew that he could count on my dad for things a handicapped father would count on from his son. Daddy, likewise, counted on Mr. Coffee for fatherly needs, especially after the death of his own father in 1964.

I recall one Wednesday night in 1966 or 1967. Although I am not certain about the year, I am certain about it being a Wednesday. Mom had picked us up from church. The Haliburton children had choir rehearsal, immediately followed by Youth Meeting every Wednesday for more than a decade. In most cases, Daddy would pick us up. In those days, one car provided all the transportation needs of families, even large families like ours. We were no exception. We were excited to see Mom behind the wheel. It was euphoric.

Wednesdays were always special to me. It was not because it was Hump Day. (That popular thought and label came later.) I loved going to church. It was an opportunity to see the friends I only got to see twice a week. I had friends at school whom I could see every day, but I had friends at church with whom I did not go to school.

The other reason Wednesdays were special to The Haliburton children was because in our house, we ate homemade hamburgers on Wednesdays. Mom had a special rectangular, iron grill that she placed across two burners. There were six round markings forged on the grill where Mom had placed time and again the ground meat patties.

I can still see the bright red tomatoes, sliced and laid out next to the green, leafy lettuce dripping water that mixed into a puddle with vinegar from the dill pickle slices. Oh yes, it was Wednesday. We were coming home from church.

We were a block away from home when we could see lights flashing from an emergency vehicle. Something serious had occurred in our neighborhood. Soon after pulling into the driveway, we got the news. Mr. Coffee had been injured on his way home when his scooter had overturned. An ambulance had been called, and he was being taken to the hospital.

Daddy had not picked us up from church because he was trying to get the sleep he needed in order to work the "graveyard shift" (12:00–8:00 AM). When we rushed around Dad's bedside to tell him that Mr. Coffee had had another accident on his scooter, Dad jumped out of bed quickly, dressed, and made his way to the scene in minutes. He returned shortly afterward with an update on Mr. Coffee's condition. Dad must have been satisfied with what he learned. I have no recollection of the details, but what I do remember leads me to believe that life returned to normal.

As a child, I thought of love as love. I suppose if I had been challenged, my understanding of love for family members would have been prioritized above my love for friends and neighbors. I loved the Coffees. Mama and Daddy loved the Coffees. Separating my love and my parents' love for the Coffees was a distinction I have no memory of understanding as a child. The Coffees were family. Daddy's care and concern for Mr. Coffee looked to me like the same care and concern on his face when he was worried about Granddaddy, his own father.

My parents had a bitter divorce. The Coffees chose a side. They had to choose. They made the easy and obvious choice. Mom had the house and the girls. We were still neighbors. The only thing that had really changed was a change for the better. There was peace at 728 Lenox. The proximity between the Coffees' house and ours was too close for them not to hear the daily arguments and the occasional fights.

The day of Mom and Dad's last fight in 1968 was the one that changed Dad's relationship with Mr. Coffee for good. Daddy would speak about it from time to time for years to come. Daddy said that Mr. Coffee's hand was shaking so bad, he was afraid Mr. Coffee might shoot him with the gun in his hand by accident.

We, Bruce, Rita, Nita, Cheryl, and I were all gathered at the apartment for the big slumber party when Dad came and told us about it afterward. As an eight-year-old girl who loved Mr. Coffee, the story was hard for me to believe the night I first heard it. It happened. Mom confirmed it when I pressed to be certain of the truth. I did not then nor have I ever to this day known my father to be a liar. Mr. Coffee, a man whom I loved and respected had threatened to shoot my daddy. It took years for me to process thoughts about the events of that evening. I do know this. I am so glad that Mr. Coffee did not kill my daddy, shoot my daddy or even shoot at my daddy.

My daddy was a good man. Time, opportunities, love, and most importantly, growing in the grace of God made him a better man. Elements that give us all a chance to change if we are alive to seize them. A split-second decision or mistake fifty years ago would have changed so much about the lives of so many. The number of victims could only be counted if the investigator could trace all the good accomplished since that time by all of the people whose lives were positively impacted by Daddy and Mr. Coffee's lives. When one man kills another, they both become victims and make victims of their loved ones. Thank God Mr. Coffee did not shoot my daddy.

Daddy lost the election for county commissioner of Precinct 3 in a run-off election. Mom got her divorce. The judge gave Mom custody of all the girls, and Dad was awarded custody of Bruce. I learned the meaning and purpose of child support. For two years after our parents' divorce, we all attended the two segregated schools in our community. Judy became the only one among us to graduate from the segregated school in our community, G. W. Carver High School. Bruce, the twins, Cheryl and I soon found ourselves completing the remainder of our K–12 educational experiences in integrated schools.

We got up early every morning to catch the bus to school. I was in the sixth grade, and the twins were in the eighth grade. We attended the same school, so we rode the same bus. It was 1970. The Federal judge had ordered La Vega ISD to implement integration in its schools. The decision from the governing board was to close the two schools in the black neighborhood, and bus the children of

Carver Park to the White elementary, intermediate, and high school in the district. Cheryl rode the bus to East La Vega Elementary. The twins and I rode the bus to La Vega Intermediate, and Bruce attended La Vega High School.

Sometimes the bus would be so crowded, students would stand in the aisle for the ride until a seat became available. The trips to and from school were cold in the winter months and hot in the months before transitioning from spring to summer and from summer to autumn. Having to stand on a crowded bus under those environmental conditions only added insult to the injury. We felt like the chattel slaves we had only read about. We joked about it after a while. Imagine how we must have looked packed to capacity on moving buses.

The twins were three years older than me, and they were docile, obedient to a fault bookworms. I was as smart as they, but I did not have the discipline for reading and studying that they had. Neither did I have their gentle nature. I was feisty, assertive. If someone pushed me, I pushed back. If someone threatened one of my siblings, the fight was mine. No questions asked. If my siblings were in a conflict, they were being picked on. They bothered no one, and they gave no reason for anyone to bother them.

When the buses were crowded, the children would sit three to a seat. Even then, some would still have to stand. Sometimes, the twins and I sat together. Other times, I would take the third seat on the edge with friends while an even more docile classmate of the twins' enjoyed my usual third seat on the edge with them. Her name was Cheryl Hicks, and we all attended church together. There were afternoon rides home from school, when the twins sat together while Cheryl and I sat together. We four always sat. I saw to that. They were fourteen. I was eleven.

Nathaniel and I were in the same science class the last period of the day. When Mr. Rogers, the science teacher, would dismiss our class, Nathaniel and I would race to the bus stop to wait for the bus. He and I were always first and second in line. Sometimes he was first. Sometimes I was, but we were always the first or second in line. One afternoon, we raced to the bus stop as usual, and I was first. As I had established by routine, I boarded the bus and saved two seats at the front of the bus. I would sit on the back of a seat and secure the seat behind it with my left foot while securing the seat I straddled with my right foot. The front seat was for the twins, and the seat immediately behind theirs was for Cheryl Hicks and me.

It happened that on this particular day, I had found a purse in "one of my seats." I was giving the purse to the driver when for some unknown reason Nathaniel decided that he was going to take one of "my seats." He grabbed my leg and tried to bend it. I was familiar with the idea of a purse being used as a weapon because I had seen the actress, Ruth Buzzi use hers many times. The first couple of times that I hit Nathaniel with the purse made the idea seem like a mistake because it was. The empty purse was made of cloth, so it was striking soft blows. I knew I had to improvise or be prepared to lose this unexpected fight. I thought to ball my hand and to hit him with my fist through the purse. It worked. The driver stopped the fight and told the administrator what Nathaniel had done. The administrator removed Nathaniel from the bus, but I was allowed to go home on the bus as usual.

Nathaniel and I lived on the same street. He would get off the bus on the first stop. The twins and I would get off on the third stop. When the bus arrived to the first stop, there stood Nathaniel's mother. She was a large, yellow-skinned woman (not jaundice, sexy), and she appeared even larger to that little eleven-year-old girl staring into her angry eyes.

When David faced Goliath, he had to think fast, but more importantly, he had to trust God. Otherwise, he did not stand a chance against the giant. Goliath was a man. David was a boy. Goliath was a warrior. David was a shepherd. Goliath was a bully. Who else would threaten the life of a boy, a good God-fearing boy? David needed God's protection. My God-fearing mind told me that I needed God's protection as I was about to face Nathaniel's mother.

The bus doors swung open, and there she stood with both hands on her hips. She asked, "Where's the little girl that was beating on my son?" For the first time, beating up Nathaniel seemed like a bad idea. Why did I have to go and fight for a seat? Nobody's going to help me now. Nathaniel's mom was calling me out.

I looked at the twins, my big sisters, for guidance. There they were, watching this drama unfold, sitting on that seat I had provided day after day and today after fighting for it. Then Nita, the younger twin spoke. She said, "Gone," like she was aggravated that it was taking me so long to identify myself. My heart sank. I knew in that instant, I had to face Nathaniel's mother. I felt betrayed. Rita and Nita were sending me out to face Goliath alone. Some big sisters they were. I would never let them fight alone, especially against a giant. Worse than that, Nita's tone had sounded judgmental, like, "Go on out there and get what you deserve." What did I ever do to her?

I could feel that the bus driver was uncomfortable with what was happening. I was searching for help wherever I could find it. Although he said nothing, the driver kept his hand on the door lever, as if he were prepared to close the door if Nathaniel's mom decided to board the bus and pull me off. I did not get off the bus, but I did stand on the top step in the doorway. Nathaniel's mom and I were face-to-face like cowboys in a western shootout. She took a look at me and asked, "Ain't you that little Haliburton girl?"

"Yes, ma'am," I answered.

She said, "Go on home. I'll be down there to talk to your mama later."

When my mother came home from work, I told her what had happened. I was afraid that my behavior was going to cause Mama to have to fight my giant. I wanted Mama to be ready. I wanted her to call the police or Aunt Olivia or her best friend, Jimmie. Mama did as she did every day after work. She got a cup of coffee, and she sat down outside in the shade to read the newspaper.

I wanted Mama to button down in the house where it was safe. Nathaniel's mom was a big woman, and she was angry. I didn't want Mama to get hurt. She was no fighter. I was the only fighter in this house, and I was afraid to fight Nathaniel's mother. Surely Mom had a plan if she was sitting in the yard, drinking coffee and reading her newspaper. I had to know what she was going to do, so I asked. Mom said, "Don't worry. She's not coming down here." Mom was right. Mom knew that Nathaniel's mother was a good neighbor. Mom knew that Nathaniel's mother was a good person. Mom knew that Nathaniel's mother was a good woman and not a violent one. Mom knew that Nathaniel's mother was not looking for trouble. They were both women with dignity and were respected women in the community. They were both mothers, and mothers understand other mothers. Whew! I know what it means to literally fight for a seat on the bus.

I have fought for love. Stanley and I were friends, and I was running short on the number of friends I had that year. I had such a polarizing personality then. Some would say still. People either liked me a lot or disliked me more. There were more in the disliked category than in the liked. Stanley and I shared the birthday month, November. Just knowing that about each other gave us an understanding between us that I was incapable of communicating to others about myself.

Stanley and I took an algebra class together. He was an athlete; basketball was his sport. I was a cheerleader. Our algebra teacher was an African American coach who would have done anything to rescue foolish black kids he thought were worth saving. Thank God for Mr. Haynes. We could not have survived integrated schools without the watchful eyes of protection and interventions of caring educators and role models like Nathaniel Haynes.

I don't know how the conflict started that day. Stanley and I had just been dismissed from algebra. He had already left the room. Whatever happened that caused Stanley and me to fight that day had already occurred. All I knew and all I needed to know before I took over the fight was what I saw when I turned that corner. I could see that Stanley had my little sister, Cheryl pinned against a wall. The look on her face told me that she was not having fun. She was in a fight.

I had no time for getting an understanding about what had taken place. I jumped right in. I felt I was doing all right until I took a punch to my nose. I wanted to quit, but I had not planned an exit strategy. The next thing I knew, a tuning rod from a flute flashed past me. Cheryl had clocked Stanley on the temple with it. Immediately a knot rose on his head.

This intervention provided enough time for Mr. Haynes to come around the corner and make sure Stanley didn't get revenge. Thanks to Mr. Haynes, Cheryl and I didn't get beat up any worse than what we did, and Stanley's injury made him look like the loser.

Stanley and I finished the school year as friends, and we remain friends today. Mr. Haynes had a talk with us after breaking up the fight, though I have no recollection of what he said. Whatever he said, it worked to reconcile my friendship with Stanley. I don't know why Cheryl and Stanley fought that day, but I know exactly why I did. I know what it means to fight for love.

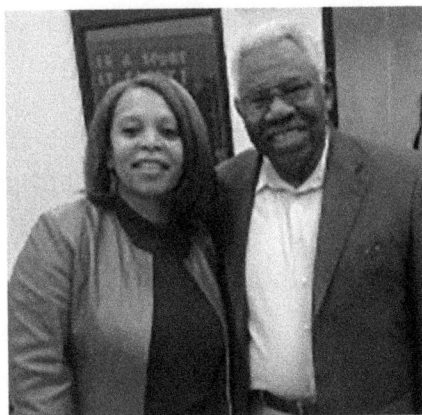

Former teacher, Mr. Nathaniel Haynes in 2018

I know what it means to be prepared and hope that you do not have to fight. I've gone to school with a pocket knife in my bra and a hammer in my purse. Instead of doing homework at night that school year, I practiced wielding a hammer. I wanted to be able to defend myself from multiple opponents in case I got jumped too. I didn't want to hurt anybody. Neither did I want anybody to hurt me. I was just a good girl—yes, a good girl, trying to survive the violent social ills found in my educational institution. I did not feel safe at school. God's mercy kept us all safe from each other. How our lives would have been different had someone gotten seriously hurt!

I have fought for money. In 1975, fifty cents was capital worth fighting about. Everybody knew that Beverly was a thief, and she would steal from a friend as quickly as she would steal from a stranger. When my fifty-cent piece came up missing, we all thought Beverly had stolen it. She denied it, but nobody believed her: not me, not the teacher, not my friends, not even my enemies. When Beverly was searched, they found money that wasn't hers, but my fifty-cent piece was not among the coins.

My peers felt bad about my not getting my money back, or so I believed. They encouraged me to fight Beverly. I didn't want to get in trouble for fighting at school, so I expressed that. Everybody understood my not wanting to get into trouble at school. They had a solution. At lunch, some students would walk to the local burger restaurant. If I went there at lunch time, I could fight her there. The school had no jurisdiction there. Problem solved.

The same helpful problem-solving peers made sure I knew that Beverly was willing to meet me there. I received threatening messages that Beverly sent, as well as those she probably did not send. I suspect Beverly even received messages from me that I did not send. The impending fight at lunch time was no longer about my fifty cents. It had evolved into something bigger. All the people from whom Beverly had stolen money and those who had other issues with Beverly and those who simply just wanted to see a fight were making plans to meet at the burger stand during lunch time.

I walked to the restaurant alone. I do not remember much about the trek. I cannot recall having second thoughts, regrets, or fear of losing. I do not believe I really had fighting on my mind. I do remember thinking that I needed to hurry back to the school before the principals could discover that I was off campus. It was not my lunch time. It was Beverly's lunch time.

I had convinced one of the teachers to let me walk to the restaurant and get her a burger. (She later told me how much she had enjoyed it.) I was her student aide. She had given me the money with which to buy her a burger. My mind was on getting her order right and getting back to the school. I waded past the crowd and placed the teacher's order.

It was a chilly day. I was wearing a brown, hand-me-down jacket that had once belonged to Rita. I went outside past the crowd once again to wait for the teacher's burger. Suddenly, I was face-to-face with Beverly on the dirt parking lot in a makeshift boxing ring that had been created hastily by a group of encircling spectators.

I don't remember what Beverly said to me before she swung at me. The fight was on. Now Beverly was about six to eight inches taller than I was. For some reason, perhaps anger about my money, I was not afraid of her. Although I did not really plan nor expect to fight her, I really did want to fight her.

My mind ventured to the last movie I had seen at the downtown theater, *Mandingo*. It was a movie about a slave who earned fame and fortune for his master by boxing. There was an extremely violent scene in the movie when the slave had to resort to biting and lacerating his opponent's throat in order to avoid being killed himself. As if on cue, Beverly bit and latched her teeth into my forehead.

My thoughts raced to the movie and shouted to me, "She's trying to kill me." I punched Beverly in the jaw, and her grip gave way. I went to work on her head. This fight was clearly no longer about a fifty-cent piece, I was fighting for my life. Who or what stopped us, I cannot say.

I got my teacher's burger order and returned to the school. The school administrators never talked as if they knew there had been a fight or as if they knew I had left campus even though it was not my lunch time. Friends would later tell me about how amazed they were by my fighting skills. The joke became, "I wonder what you would have done to her if you had taken your coat off."

Shamefully, I later found the missing fifty-cent coin exactly where I had hidden it from thieves and from myself. By the time I had matured enough in life to admit this wrong and to apologize to Beverly, she had been dead a couple of years. We all graduated in 1977. She was the first casualty after graduation. Her untimely death reminded us all about how much fun she was. Suddenly, we all declared how much we loved her and would miss her.

I know what it means to fight for money.

My senior year in high school, I lost a fight I had for my dignity in a moment of anger. I never had a chance to throw a punch; neither did Kathy. The principal was standing there, and we were all three engaged in a simple, civil conversation. When the mood changed to battle stations, the principal responded with speed and precision. He pushed me hard enough to be considered being thrown to the ground, and he grabbed Kathy. By the time I got back on my feet, an assistant principal had me and was escorting me to the office.

Kathy and I had been best friends for a year. She had spent the night at my house a few times. We played cards together, against others and we had cheated each other at playing cards when we couldn't find anyone who wanted to play and lose to us. If I had money, we had money and vice versa. Everybody at school knew that we were friends, so all were in shock about what happened that day.

My senior year was a busy one like all high school students on track to graduate. Most of us girls weighed between 100 and 120 pounds. We were wearing makeup and looking our best every day. We were behaving and presenting ourselves in respectful manners because we wanted to be engaged by adults as adults. This was a transformation from the junior in high school who had been best friends with Kathy the previous year.

Kathy was still the same. She was several shades darker than I was. She weighed nearly twice what I weighed. She was fluffy and as jolly-looking as she was jolly. She wore a tiny, neat afro that was the biggest source of the reason she was bullied. It was her sportsmanship in managing the bullying that probably first caught my attention. Once we became friends, the bullying stopped although the nickname stuck. I was one of the few people who did not refer to Kathy as, "Kojak."

In the late 1970s, a television series featured a topnotch New York detective named Kojak. The detective's character was played by an actor named Telly Savalas. Savalas was completely and distinctly bald. Kathy had been dubbed Kojak.

I do not know what Kathy and I were feuding about that day. One minute we were talking to the principal. The next minute we were in the office waiting to be suspended. I do know that I had had the last word. As was my custom and skill, I was quite satisfied that it had established my academic superiority and level of maturity over my former best friend and in front of our principal.

In response, because she had no comeback words, Kathy took a deep breath and blew it in my face. That's when I lost my fight against my dignity. I was so competitive then, so determined to win, so bent on having the one-up, I took the one-up opportunity that came to my mind first. She blew in my face, so I spat in hers. One of the most despicable and unlady-like things a teenaged girl can do, I did. I regret that to this day.

I waited a split second for her reaction, but it was delayed. I turned to walk away because I was ashamed of myself. We were all three in shock. Kathy charged at me like a bull. The principal blocked her, threw me to the ground and grabbed her. We were both taken to the office. We were only sent home for the remainder of the day.

I was so angry. I was angry at Kathy for blowing in my face, but I was even angrier because she had made me angry enough to lose my dignity. The principal never thought as highly of me after that incident. I know what it means to fight for pride but instead lose my dignity.

I have been successful in my career with using my fighting experiences with discouraging others from fighting. Some students find satisfaction with just expressing what they want to say to their rivals in a supervised environment. Bullies need to be held accountable for their behavior and to be warned of the consequences for refusing to submit to safety expectations in the presence of their victims. Through talking about their conflict, many students discover that the problem they had with each other was the creation of a third party who had pitted them against each other with lies. My personal favorite technique is teaching girls to avoid fighting while saving face among their peers by simply declaring, "I am too cute to be fighting." The statement serves as comic relief during a moment of heightened tension. Students must be taught to use their words and not their hands to solve their conflicts.

Take Us with You

Take us with you.
Find something for us to do
That will make it necessary for us
To reach the next level of progress too.

Please don't leave us behind
Struggling to find our own way
To survive.
We did not choose to arrive in
Your World of High Stakes Competition.

You have forced us to petition
To access what is our right to possess.
We have endured violence.
We have forgiven
Those who trespassed against us,
Century after century
Believing that eventually
We would be allowed
To catch up
To keep up
To reach up
When it's time to
Go up to the next level of success.
Stop blocking our progress.
Take us up too.

Whispers

Now, I find myself whispering about
How I feel about the things
I disagree with you about.
I feel as though you are
Out to get me, so
You can forget me and
Leave me behind,
But I will not let you.
The Dream binds our fate.
Our country will never be great
As long as you treat me
Like you hate me or
Like you hate that I am here.
You fear me because
You don't understand me.
You never will until you deal
With welcoming me
To join your journey to success.
I am not impressed with your laws
Designed to cause me
To stay in a place
That helps you feel
Safe and out of my social reach
You want to teach me a lesson?
Teach me how to be a blessing.
Teach me that I have value within.

Teach me that the color of my skin
Truly does not matter to you.
Teach me that I can honestly
Express what I think about
What you say and the things you do
Without retribution from you.
I've got to be me.
It's my right to be free
From your judgment just because
I am different.
Accept me and let me
Tell you when you are wrong.
Don't make me feel that I must go along
If I am to get along
Otherwise, I can no longer belong
Among those who get your respect.
Collect my thoughts.
Collect my feelings.
Collect my dreams.
Collect my assessments and
Place them among the rest of
The thoughts, feelings, and dreams
You cherish.
Measure what I treasure.
Allow volume for my whisper
Without blisters from your scorn.

It Is Not All Our Fault

Much of what is wrong with my community
Is not all the fault of my people.
Your fathers should have thought
About the consequences of
Cultural devastation
From one generation to the next.
Yet your regrets don't come close
To those most of us have about
What we see happening to our children.

You call us Americans too
But make us feel like foreigners
Who must be tolerated.
You obliterated our language.
Our forefathers used stories
In our native home
To cool the anguish of their sons.
Your fathers dared our fathers
To use their tongues to correct their sons.

Instead, your fathers used whips,
Ropes, and knives
To deny the enslaved a choice
Whether or not to obey.
Once the law no longer gave permission
To use cruel weapons of submission
It was too late to use tradition
To communicate the self-destruction
Caused by hate and a bitter, raging heart
Bent on vengeance.

As much as we would like to halt
The senseless violence and
Our lack of unity
For getting things done
Most of what is wrong with our community
Is not our fault
And we cannot fix it on our own.

Search My Eyes

Search my eyes.
Will you find the answers that you seek?
Will they betray me and convey to you
The inner turmoil
I have struggled
All my life to conceal?
Will they guide you through
The tunnel of my colored skin
To reveal the hiding place of my soul?
Go ahead,
Search my eyes, and I
I will search yours.

Nobody Like Me

I watched TV as a child trying to find
Somebody like me
Who was living the American dream
I thought I had a right to live.
But there was nobody like me there.

I saw Cosby on *I Spy*
And the black guy on *Mission Impossible*
And I wondered if it were possible
For a black man
To work above ground or
To ever get the girl
Showcased as the prize.

If nobody like me could get the girl on TV
And black men were seen in magazines
Seeking treatment to live as white men to be happy
Then I knew there was something wrong
With my mother's account of the world.
Among all the happy, successful people
In the real world
There was nobody like me.

Winners

The color of your skin
Automatically made you a winner
When you entered this world or
So you were made to think
By those who linked
Being born white with
Being blessed by the God
In whom America trusts.

Those of us with skin of color must
Teach each new generation
That the rule of law in our nation
Protects the equalization expectations of
Men and women of all races.

It is the virtuous content of character that
Automatically makes winners
Not white skin.
The sooner we all, whether
Red, yellow, black, brown, or white
Begin truly living by this creed
The better off we shall all be.

Then and only then will we no longer need
To question the arrogant look of
Privilege and supremacy
Masked in your face but
Clearly visible in the faces of your children.
As they develop the language and
Countenance that conceals that
Every lesson you taught them
In what you said about people of color,
Every lesson you taught them
In how you behaved
Towards men and women of color,
Every decision you taught them to make
Based on your interactions with
Americans of color,
Taught them that being born white
Automatically gave them might and
Made them right and exempt from
The plight of people of color.

Your forefathers cared little about
How they made our forefathers feel and
Until you are honest with yourself
Your privileged mind-set will
Continue appealing to your children.
People of color will never heal
From the stigma that plagues us at birth
When whites act like, talk like, and
Make decisions like and
Treat us like
White skin is automatically worth more
Than all other skins of color.

Granddaddy, Edwin Haliburton

The Question

Take a simple test.
Your answer will provide the best
Insight into your depths of prejudice.
You will find a hidden message
Coded just for you.
If the power to choose were granted
To those of you whose skin
Lack the ebony hue
Which would you select to have
White skin or
To have America elect
A black, you
The United States President?

Quit Trying to Fit

Quit trying to fit
Into places that were
Designed to keep you out.
I doubt that
You will ever fit
Even into the outer reaches of
The white man's empire.

Even those who believe
They are colorblind
Find that they still
Have color vision
When it comes to penalties
Positions, marriage, and money.

So when you're treated like a token
And you find yourself hoping
That one day
Your colorblind associates will see
That you fit right in.
You should just give up
Trying to blend
Among the other shades of skin.
Because in a tight
The colorblind still see
In black and white.

Always on the Outside Looking In

Always on the outside
Looking in as a child
My poor, White Gramps
Learned the culture of
Those wild with wonder
Blacks with businesses of their own.
Whiskey, women, and words in painful tunes
Sang about and
Danced out
In black taverns that welcomed those
Who spoke the language of rejection and despair
No matter what color they were.

Gramps worked hard and with enough success
He received an invitation to the Bigots' nests.
They welcomed him to come inside and see.
We do not speak their language here
Except in laughter, jokes, and jeers.
They told him
Leave your love for them
Before you enter in.

Gramps entered the bigots' lair and took a look around
He was so surprised by what he found.
Their whispers, gossip, and smirks
Could not heal his heartache and hurts
Like the whiskey, women, and warriors
In black red-light district bars.
It was there that Gramps felt peace.
He could relax and feel at ease.
He could drink, shoot pool, and laugh
Without being judged.

Gramps had been on the outside looking in.
Bigots had allowed him to enter but
He returned again and again
Seeking solace among black Americans he knew
Would never have a chance to see.
And they knew from his presence
Without one word from him
That the business on their inside
Their exhausted, bitter insides
Left Gramps still on the outside
Looking in, yet somehow satisfied.

The Prophet's Voice

Listen, Generation, and
You will hear the
Voice of your prophets
Declaring your destiny
Measured in time
But more often
Measured in a series of
Signs of the times.

Africa cried
As the Creator summoned
Her sons and daughters
Robed in chains
To scout new wonders
In a distant land.
"Go, He ordered
Meet your brother there.
Though cruel at first he'll seem
He will change when he sees
That you too are my son
And you shall have your part.

Serve your brother bound
While I soften his heart
With words that give him peace.
And in return
You'll live free with him
As you lived free
Before he took you
From your first home."

The prophet called
And told Abe Lincoln
It was time.
Before you leave
Release your brother's chains.
Teach him to read
So King will know their rights.
Leave him not only free
But also free to lead.

Bobby and John will help
To bear the light of truth
And then at last,
The last will be the first.
The prophet's voice said
Give him forty years and
Africa's son will
Shatter the glass
Above his head.

The prophet spoke
But America's voice was heard.
Oh, Africa,
It's time to show
The world your son.
The night he won
Africa wept again
But tears of joy had
Replaced the tears of pain.

Stand in My Shoes

Stand in my shoes
Before you judge me.
View the vicious struggle
From my vantage.
Feel my anguish.
Confront my doubt.
Fight my self-contempt.
Face my fear.
Endure and survive as
I have.
Stand in my shoes
Before you judge me.
Then you can teach me
To laugh at your jokes
Jokes that only made this
Militant, violent, nigger, coon
Want to punch you in the nose
As soon as you called this rose something
That was unable to stop me from
Smelling just as sweet.

Slip on my African feet; then
Force them into the European shoes
I must wear to make you comfortable.
Then stand there powerless and defeated
Before you judge me.
Stand there in my shoes
Knowing that the clothes you wear
The words you speak
The books you read
The ambitions and desires you have
Belong to another because
The court and the rules
To protect or reject you
Are his.
So stand in my shoes
Before you judge me.

Be Good

When good people do bad things
They may be seen and judged to be bad.
If you have had enough of
Pretending to be rough and too tough
To be told what to do
Stop sending messages that misrepresent how you
Want to be known.
Your behavior determines where you belong,
Whether among the good, the bad, or the ugly-acting.
You could find yourself right back in
The same position that you were
Wishing not to be in before.
Doors open for good people, but are
Closed in the faces of those
Who have wasted their lives
Being bad, not just doing bad things
As even good people sometimes do.
You must decide
Who you will show yourself to be.
We want to see you as good.

Inside and Out

She is beautiful inside and out
Though I doubt that many are able
To look past the negative labels
Placed on her by others.
She covers them with her smile and
Every once in a while
She feels that only furious, blind anger will
Protect her from people who just don't understand.
If only the good in her heart
Could land her a fresh start
Somewhere, where she won't be prejudged
Somewhere, where gentle, loving words can nudge her
Towards doing what
She already knows is right to do.
May she someday, some way
Find a place
Where she'll have nothing to prove or work out
Except that she is beautiful inside and out.

I Want to Learn

Teach me. I want to learn.
I get tired of waiting my turn
For your attention.
You let disrupters
Get the time
You should use to teach me.
Choose me.
Who's addressing
The reason I come to school?
I never act a fool.
I am here every day
Ready to learn.
Show some concern
For my academic needs.
I want to succeed.
Failing class clowns are relieved
When they get you to fail too.
Do not fail to teach me.
I want to learn.

Erica

I taught Erica when she was a ninth grader. She was in my English class. She was a diamond in the rough. She and her classmates would waste precious class time arguing and disturbing the learning environment. I would have to stop teaching and manage discipline.

I don't remember the particular literary piece we were studying, but I do remember the day Erica's class was forever transformed and began developing a learning culture. I always believed in allowing my students an opportunity to share personal experiences that connected their lives to my lessons.

That day, Erica shared a heart-wrenching, dramatic story about the death of her brother. Her brother had been shot and murdered. Two cars trapped him in the drive-through of a What-a-Burger. She was in tears, and she left others in the class in tears as well. Prior to her emotional finish, she and another girl had had a bitter exchange that could have erupted into a fight between them. Darrell put his hand over Erica's mouth to silence her and stop the argument. Erica snatched Darrell's hand off her mouth. The tension between Erica and the girl subsided, and Erica's anger was turned toward Darrell. Suddenly, Darrell put his hand up to his nose and gave a moan as though Erica's breath had made his hand stink. The class, including Erica and the girl, burst into laughter. A bond among the students in the class was created that lasted the remainder of the school year.

Fast forward to a day when Erica's son was in the eleventh grade and attending the high school where I was one of eight assistant principals. Erica's son had gotten into trouble after defending his girlfriend who had been attacked by another male student. Erica came to the school every day to protest the campus's policy for the consequences of her son's behavior. Her son had become frustrated and wanted her to concede, but she would not relent. She believed that she was right and that the school's decision was wrong.

For three days, I listened to Erica yell and scream in the offices of three of my colleagues, trying to convince them to change her son's consequences. She would not give up. She repeated her defense over and over and over again. She got louder with each round and became more and more frustrated, and the more frustrated she became, the louder she got. It reminded me of listening to the desperation in her voice when she was in my ninth grade classroom. By the third day, I could take no more of her yelling.

I had kept my distance from the situation. I had seen the video and had determined that Erica's son was wrong and had been assigned the appropriate consequence for his actions. I had never seen nor heard a parent as persistent as Erica was being. I was disappointed in her and her behavior. I felt that I knew her well enough to be able to intervene, help her accept the campus's policy and give up her crusade to reverse her son's consequences.

I went into my colleague's office and inserted myself into the conflict. I carefully listened to her story for the first time. I saw her point. She was right. I did not have the authority to reverse the consequences of Erica's son, but I was willing to be the advocate for her cause. I had the communication skills necessary to help the principal understand the point she had been arguing for three days. The principal agreed. Erica was right. She made her voice be heard the only way she knew how. She did not threaten to use violent behavior. She did not use profanity. She was loud because she was a desperate mother.

Desperate Mom

I will scream.
I will yell.
I will tell you
Over and over
Until you listen and
Not just because I
Want my way.
Today, I am in this fight
Because I know
I am right and
You are wrong.
I am ready to argue
With you as long as it takes
For you to understand
That my demands are based
On the facts in my particular case.
There are exceptions to every rule, and
You fuel my passion
To communicate my cause
Because your laws do not apply
This time.
This is the exception, and
I am not accepting,
"No" for an answer
Without a fight.

I will talk to him.
I will talk to her.
I will talk to you
Until I finally
Get through to
Someone who actually hears
What I have to say.
I will whisper.
I will point.
I will use my hands
But I won't be a threat.
I will not let
You forget that
I am not satisfied.
My rights, when I'm right,
Will not be denied in peace.
I will raise my voice.
I will raise my hands.
I will take a stand, and
You will find
That I was right
The entire time.

Fight Me

Fight me.
I have a right
To use your face for
My punching bag.
I have had enough of you
Other things and other people
Who frustrate me
Day after day
Making me feel that
There is no other way
To deal with the
Mess my life is in.
I have nothing to lose, so
Let's fight when you are ready.
I have plenty of petty reasons
From which to choose.
I have nothing to lose
Except this fight with you.
It might make you
Feel better too.
I'll punch you.
You'll punch me.
I'll help you and hopefully
You can give me the help I need

FRANCENE HALIBURTON-FRANCIS, ED.D.

To see that
Fighting is a waste of time.
Fighting cannot unwind the
Tangles in my life.
I have no right to blame another
For the fears,
I need to fight within myself.
There is nothing left, but
For me to fight me.
There is nothing left
To free me but for me to
Fight me.

The Girl Who Needed Love

I was tired. It had been a long, dramatic weekend. Daylight Savings Time had taken its toll. I was determined to return to work on Monday on time despite the scheduled early morning meeting. I dragged along all day, but I made it. I had a relaxing dinner and evening with my husband. I believe he was surprised that I retired for the evening so early. I couldn't help it. I was exhausted to the point of becoming ill.

The next morning, when the alarm went off, I felt I was still in dire need of sleep. After hitting the Snooze button on the clock for the second time, I felt there was only one solution. I texted the members of the campus administrative team. I told them that I would not be in for another couple of hours. I did not feel as though a couple of additional hours would give me adequate rest, but I felt that it would be enough rest to motivate me at least to get dressed and out of the house. I closed my eyes. I thought about the responsibilities of my job, particularly the responsibilities in which I take personal care.

I do not like bully behavior, especially in a school setting. Parents have a right to expect their children to be able to attend school in a safe learning environment. Students have a right to feel that school personnel will protect them from physical harm and that goes for harm from known bullies. I attended an unsafe school my ninth grade year. The administrators, teachers and other staff members were afraid of the campus bullies, and the bullies knew it. We, the students, felt we had no choice but to resort to measures to protect ourselves. I learned through the experience of that year, how important it is for administrators to do their jobs in managing campus safety effectively. I also determined that cafeteria workers, custodians and bus drivers are not exempt from bearing some responsibilities for assuring the safety of all students in their care. Few things motivate me to get to work like recalling my commitment to providing a safe learning environment for all, especially the most vulnerable.

It was a similar thought about students being safe that motivated me to get to work this particular morning. However, it was not a thought about a school setting. This morning, I was motivated by a violent attack I had seen posted on Facebook before going to bed the previous night. What I had seen disturbed my rest. I went to sleep that night praying for the stranger I had seen on the video, being brutally beaten. She reminded me of so many high school girls I see every day.

The victim in the video was a short teenaged African American girl between the ages of fourteen and sixteen. Her skin was brown. She had long braids that flowed to her waist weaved into her head. The video begins with her walking down the street with a friend on a beautiful, sunny day. She was wearing shorts and her outfit was matched to give her the attractive look she was likely seeking. She was wearing sandals. I inferred from her prance that she was pleased with her appearance.

Suddenly, a car pulled up near her and two African American young ladies, aged between seventeen and nineteen, got out and one of them confronted the younger teenager. The older girl got the attention of the younger girl with a barrage of profanity and threats. The younger girl turned around and began twisting her braids up into a ball as if to prepare for a fight.

She seemed to be the only one surprised and unprepared for a physical conflict. (The cell phone's camera was cued early enough to capture the bully's arrival by vehicle.) The poor girl had no hope of avoiding the attack. When she let go of the bundle of braids in order to use her hands to defend herself, the long locks were seized by the older bully.

The younger, smaller girl was flung to the pavement. The sound of her body hitting the concrete was captured by audio, as well as the gasps and responses of the spectators. The bigger bully swung the girl around by her hair, punched her repeatedly, pulled the younger girl's head downward by her weave and kneed her in her face. The young girl fell to the ground again, and the bully kicked her in the face. The post ended there.

Many thoughts wandered through my mind about this incident I had viewed. My first thought was about the unfortunate, countless number of times scenes like this one have played out in the lives of so many victims. I wondered what the girl could have said or done to make the young lady who beat her in the video so angry with her. I have been angry enough with people to imagine delivering such a beating, but I could never be that heartless and vicious, even in anger. Whatever the victim had done, the beating she received was inexcusable.

I was concerned about the small children who were incidentally filmed in the background who had witnessed the violent attack. Why weren't these children with such impressionable minds not living lives among adults who loved them enough to shelter them from such a display of barbaric behavior? I wondered what happens in the lives of children going forward in their lives after they witness scenes of violence once, twice, maybe even more times than I can imagine. How does witnessing this type of rage impact children mentally and emotionally? What are the long term affects in their everyday lives which also include their daily lives and interactions at school?

I wondered how the cameraperson and others watching, specifically her friend with whom she had been walking in the beginning of the video, could be heartless enough not to put a stop to the fight. I wondered how much longer the fight continued and hoped that it had ended when the video posting ended. I worried about the extent of the girl's injuries. I wondered if the experience would change her in a way that would make her a better person or a worse one or not change her at all.

How many times are scenes like this one or worse repeated in African American neighborhoods all over the United States? I had to go to work and fight against this behavior becoming the norm. Education is the way to avoid a lifestyle like this. The cold, hard, unfortunate truth is that for many, violence is a lifestyle. I had so many questions about the young girl who reminded me of the many young African American girls I see every day.

Who loves her? Will the people who love her want to retaliate (an urge I would have to work hard to fight) or would they feel that she had gotten what she deserved? Had she been betrayed, so the ambush could take place? Had she learned that she needs to change the course her life was on? Did she have anybody to talk to in order to get past this experience? Was there someone who loves her enough to show her the patience she would need to change? I had to go to work, so I could continue my crusade against violent lifestyles and to use the power of my position on my campus to protect victims from those who do not hesitate to engage in violent behavior.

Violence is not required to defeat violence. Character education has the power to overcome physical violence. I defeat violence nearly every day, and I do it without physical confrontation. I have seen both males and females change their lives from ones of violence just because a conversation finally had inspired them to think about their choices in managing conflicts. I had to go to work, so I could do my job.

Weaved Hair

Weave me a head full of hair.
I don't care if
My own will no longer grow.
I know the weave will leave
Rows and rows of damaged follicles,
No longer able to produce a root.
Just do it.
Give me long, thick locks
That may block me from remembering
My reality and developing wisdom and
Healthy truths that youth need to know
Before pursuing outer beauty.
Skin-deep beauty and no beauty within
Is no match for
Beauty that begins inside
Where who we really are resides.
I am more than
The person others see
When they look at me, but
I don't care
As long as they see me
Wearing lots of long weaved-in hair.

Pain Relief

It pains us to see
From the halls of eternity
What you've done to the place
We slaved for you to have
Among the human race
In these United States.
Does it no longer matter to you
All the things we had to go through
To come from no choice at all to
All the same choices as the boy in blue?
Blond hair, blue eyes, outfitted in blue
To match the skies that he believed
To be the limits of his lofty heights,
The master soared from our sights
But not from yours.
So, son, take the rights you've gained and
Climb higher than the territory you've claimed
Climb until nothing remains for you to achieve.
Make haste and
Relieve the pain
Your behavior has caused us all.

Demand Respect

You demand respect, but
You don't seem to get
That cussing out and
Shouting at others
Will only bring you trouble.
Obey rules and laws.
Then there will be no cause
To correct the things you say or do
With malicious intent.
You can prevent most of
The consequences assigned to you
If you would only learn to do
What is right to do.
Be kind, respectful, and helpful.
Make an effort to be successful
At earning respect.
Invest a little of it every day.
You will soon discover a better way
To gain the respect you profanely say
You demand.

You Are Still a Child

You're still a boy.
You're just a boy
Who acts like
He just got a new toy
Because he's expecting
A baby by a girl
Who is still just a girl.
What kind of world
Can you expect to provide
For a baby to reside in
When you can't even
Decide what is and what is not
Appropriate for a child to do?
Just look at what you've gotten yourself into.

It might be a while
Before you realize how deep
The mess you're in is
Because you, yourself are still a child, but
After a while,
You will be a man.
Then you will understand
How we can still see
The boy you think is gone.
We acknowledge all that
You can do on your own, but
We still realize you are not grown.
You are still a child.

Don't Stop

Be strong.
People will do you wrong and
Talk to you like
You don't belong to the human race, but
No one can replace
How special you are,
How great you were created to be.
Bullies waste time
Trying to get a laugh at your expense.
It may not make sense now,
But given time,
You will see how
The sad, pathetic life of a loser
Turns out.
Stay straight and strong from
The inside out.
There is no doubt
You will win in the end.
Even your loser bully wishes
For the wonderful future
You are destined to have.
You are headed for the top.
Don't stop.

My Space

My space is the place
Where I go to escape
The people, places and things
That make me want to
Blow my top in anger
Before I do.

My space is the place where
You can find me
Quietly shedding tears
In hope that
No one else hears
The longings in my heart.
My space is the place
Where I start to think
Things are not
As bad as they seem.
In my space
Things improve.

My space is the place
Where I go to create
Big dreams
Dreams too big for
Others to believe
That I can achieve.
In my space
I am great.

Wisdom

Wisdom wants your decision
About the path you want to take.
Make up your mind
To find the way
That leads to success.
Your happiness depends on
The behaviors you choose.
You can win or
You can lose.
You can be kind or be mean.
You can be seen doing
Helpful or hateful things.
You can show others compassion or
Let your actions
Be cruel and beautiless.
People with wisdom
Demonstrate peace.
Wise people release
Their need for revenge and
Embrace a life
Full of forgiveness and love.
Make your decision.
Live a life of wisdom.

Watch What You Say

Watch what you say.
You may regret the way
People who hear your words
Treat you afterwards.
You may think you don't care
But you need to
Beware more than dogs in life.
Heed my warning.
Your attitude and lack of gratitude
Will return and smack you in your face.
You waste entire days
Thinking of ways to get what you want
At someone else's expense and
Then have the nerve to resent
Their correction, guidance, and advice.
Precisely what future results do you expect
When you've made no effort to connect yourself
To the people, places, and things
Capable of helping you to achieve
Dreams that seem impossible today.
So please,
Watch what you say.

Not Hirable

You are not hirable.
Your skills are undesirable
For an environment designed for work.
You know how to use words to hurt others.
You know how to lie and
Put it on your mother's life.
You know how to announce that
You don't feel like working.
You know how to pounce on anyone
Who dares to encourage you to work.
You know how to ignore work.
You know how to
Play, laugh, joke, and clown around.
You know how to explain
Why you're doing whatever you're doing
Instead of doing what you should be doing.
You know how to complain about how
Everybody is treating you so wrong
But no one has caused you more harm
Than you have caused yourself.
Your skills are undesirable, and
You are not hirable.

Trying to Reach You

You can't read.
You can't write, but
You are bold enough
To bite the hands of those
Who try to teach you.
Your life is headed for disaster.
Cast your dreams
Far beyond any means
You have of achieving them
From where you stand today.
Make demands of yourself
So you won't be left behind.
You and your loved ones
Act like you're winning a game.
You have blamed those
You've yelled at
Cussed and fussed at,
For your illiteracy.
You have taken every environment
Designed for you to learn and
Turned it into a circus act
Since first grade.
Then you have the nerve to attack
The teachers who have made every possible effort
To reach you.

Listen

Listen,
So you can learn
What must be done
To turn the corner on
The problems that we face
Within the African American race.
Break the cycle of madness.
Take the control.
Unfold your arms and
Stop ignoring the mess
Being dropped at your door.
The violence and ignorance
Create an expense
We can no longer afford.
Listen.
Then decide what
You can do to help.
Are you listening?
Listen.

She Is Not the One

She is not the one.
Just think about
The way she makes you feel.
When love is real,
She is not satisfied until
You are as happy over her
As she is over you.
She will do whatever it takes
To bring a smile to your face.
She will not frustrate you.

She is not the one.
She makes you angry enough
To behave dangerously and
She does it intentionally
Because she does not care.
Beware of girls like that.
Attack your feelings for her
Instead of anything or anyone else.
Be good to yourself.
Wait for the right girl
To come into your life.
Trust me. Believe me.
She is not the one.

The Game of Self

These youth foolishly face fate boldly.
They say coldly, "I don't care," and
Some won't care even after
The laughter is long gone from their lives.
They deceive themselves and
Believe deep within
That they suffer due to the decisions of others.
They blame mothers, missing fathers, sisters, brothers, and
All who refuse to cover the costs of
The consequences of their choices just one more time.
They whine about who should be blamed
Once no willing victims are left to play their
Game of Self such that they somehow get to win.
They live their lives without regret because
They choose to forget that the Universe has laws
That will not let them
Set the price of the pain they purchase with reckless living.
They never realize that those who forgive them
Over and over do so because they care.
Being bold is really good should our youth decide
To listen to their elders to learn
Why they keep missing the prize.
The eyes of the elders were once young and
Even the elders have done foolish things boldly,
Ignoring the warning calls of all who loved them too,

Choosing rather to do as they pleased.
When the elders were young, they too believed that
They could change the ending and they
Would wind up winning the Game of Self
That left their elders looking like losers.
But they loss too.
Each new group of youth fall prey
To the same ending.
The young are called because they are strong.
Strong and bold combined create power.
To tower above your young peers
Learn to be wise beyond your years.
Let wise men mentor and guide you
Away from Fate who awaits
The youth who boldly challenge him.
Now that you've been told the truth, bold youth,
Whom will you blame
When you lose while playing
The Game of Self?

A Good Life

The youth I try to reach
Do not understand the truth
About the power of choice.
They have a voice they want heard
But fail to choose words
That force others to hear
What they say with respect.
These youth let foolish
Projects
Interfere with
Where their lives can lead.

Whether they will fail or succeed
In the days and years ahead
Often depends on what is said and done
Today.
Say what you mean and
Mean what you say but
Be sure that what you say
Conveys thoughtful words of wisdom.
Otherwise, the system will take your voice and
Your power of choice.
If what you say and what you do
Threatens to harm another
You will pay a price
Young sister, young brother.
Follow good instructions and
Only good instructions
For a good life!

Get Out of the Game

Get out of the game
My brother
No one will blame you
If you do.
There are no rules for players to know
Because they are created
As players go through each fight.
Players must fight for their right
To survive and stay in the game.
Some have to fight to stay alive.
Losers lay dead where
Their hearts stop or
They are eliminated from the game
Once they're handcuffed by the cops.
You are no creator, Player.
You have no chance of winning.
Like I said
In the beginning
Get out of this game
Before you too
Wind up maimed, dead, or
Locked up for life.

A Gun?

Why do you need a gun?
Whether a fake or a real one?
What do you need a gun to express
That your words cannot impress
Upon another if given time?
Guns and trouble travel together.
When they meet, at least two
Lives are forever changed.
I find it strange
That you should need a gun?
Would you risk your life
When you've only just begun to live?

Disobedience

Disobedience may be the
Most expedient means of
Getting your way but
It is a form of disrespect and
You can expect a consequence or two
No matter what your intent.
To prevent penalties' unpleasantness and
To live your life with less distress
Don't break rules
Just to get what you want quickly.
Learn instead
To quickly obey what is right to do.
Disobedience
No matter the reason
Will only create problems for you.

Losers Don't Fit

You no longer feel you fit, and
You wish your loved ones would quit
Expecting you to accept responsibility
For the mess in your reality.
Your competition is wishing
To never cross your path
For you are so lost from
The Checkpoints that determine
Whose lives thrive and
Who dies lost in disgrace.
You no longer fit
Where others are serious and curious
About learning facts from myths.
You have missed out on
So much of what counts.
You don't have an ounce of sense and
You're too dense to listen to
The teacher, the preacher, and
All who try to reach you inside
Your Lost World of Losers

Where you are a star.
You want to play.
You want to have fun.
You want to prey upon anyone
You perceive to be too weak
To beat you at the
Loser games you love to play,
Games that you can win.
When you win at Loser Games
You are a loser just the same.
You're so much a loser and user of
Lying, violent, thieving, disrespectful
Heathen, losing tools
You don't even know the reason
You no longer fit.

The Curse

Allow me to rehearse
The consequences of being cursed
With the heart to succeed
But you never learned to write or to read
Well enough to negotiate the terms of your life.
You will need more than an imagination.
You will need a formal education
If you expect to "get paid"
For what you are able to do.
Those who hire, fire, and promote
Will note that you are unteachable
And a diploma or degree was unreachable
Because you were distracted
By the follies of fool's gold
Despite being told that you were making a mistake.
You will wait in line and
As time passes you by for better days
You will be stuck showing others
Ways to get promoted to higher grounds.
You will hang around hoping that
Having experience and heart
Will be enough to earn you a chance to advance
But they won't be.
Believe me,
The curse is so much worse than
You want to know.

Do Not Steal, Kill, or Destroy

Do not become the toy
Used by the one who
Comes to steal, kill, and destroy.
He is a loser with a horrible future.
Misery loves company but
The level the devil is destined to suffer
Will be tougher than he or
Any other can withstand
Alone or with another.
There is no love in Hell's pit.

Do not take what does not belong to you.
Work, search, ask, and do
What it takes to make you happy
While keeping a good name.
Tame your reckless anger again
So when you feel an impulse
To kill another and steal away his life,
You can stop and take the time to think.
Sync your soul into the sufferings endured
By your ancestors in the past.
To live, they had to cast their angers aside,
Forgive the unforgettable deeds against humanity
They were forced to helplessly witness, yet
They maintained their sanity and destroyed nothing.
The thing for you to do is likewise
If you too are to stay alive.
Otherwise, a terrible fate awaits you.

Cuffs, Shackles, and Bars

Cuffed hands can't clap
To express a joyous emotion.
Neither can they motion
For a celebration to begin.
When hands get cuffed
Someone has had enough
With their efforts
To steal, kill, and/or destroy.
Cuffed hands cannot be
Lifted high with pride.

Shackled feet can neither drive nor ride
To be by the side of a dying loved one
Without feeling shameful regrets
Deep in the heart.
The eyes of shackled feet weep
While the mind of shackled feet
Recalls all the times
They got away before the day
They got caught and learned
How shackles halt feet and
Keep them from leaping up with joy.

Jail bars are never going to need a map.
Those behind bars never have to answer
The question, "Where you at?"
They nap, sleep, read, pee, and weep
All within the same few feet
Day after day.
They may take some time to think about
The places they won't go
Should they get out.
Bars limit travel.
So no car, no gas, no problem
Getting where you need
To be today or tomorrow.
The walks to the bars
Are not far away.

If handcuffs, shackles, and bars
Are not appealing to you
Don't cause the laws
To be on the lookout for you
Because of the things you do or don't do.

Fun

Have fun, but
Remember that the reason
You come to school is to learn.
The way to turn your life
From its present situation
Is to get an affordable education
Beyond high school.
A college degree is like a precious jewel.
It has value.

Have you listened and paid attention and
Increased your comprehension in the lessons
That your teachers struggle past disrupters to teach?
Diplomas prove that you are reachable.
Degrees tell employers you are teachable
Because they don't have money to waste
Figuring out whether or not
You have what it takes
To make it on the job.
The people they hire to work
Must be worth what employers are willing to pay.
They will teach you
Some of what you need to know but
They expect you to come
Already knowing a great deal

Before you even fill out an application.
Your diploma, your degree
Help employers see
That hiring you is not a waste of time.
They take no diploma or degree as a sign
That you have trouble completing tasks and
A person like that is among the last type
They choose to employ.
A person not used to working or
Searching for solutions or
Enduring retribution,
Unwilling to sacrifice for success
Only concerned with short-lived happiness
That person is undesirable
To the people able to hire them.
Make up your mind
Not to waste the time
You are provided
To learn at school.
You'll be glad
When what you know
Opens employment door after
Door after door for you.
That's fun.

Respect Life

Love and respect Life and value all
Who have been called to breathe and
To have a heartbeat.
Take care that you not stain your hands with blood.
You will reap what you sow
Even if it takes decades for it to grow and take revenge.
When did pain become a joke
To provoke males to bond closer together?
When did it become better to bully the weak
Rather than to seek ways to
Keep my brother, my sister safe?
How does living on the run become fun
To someone with a right
To pursue the American dream?
It seems you are confused about
The things that used to give us pride.
You shame my history and
Make me more a mystery
To be segregated and isolated
Rather than appreciated and understood.
I wish you would simply try
My suggestions to tone down your aggressions.
You are not the first.
You have not been treated the worst.
Your claims are not unknown.

If you want permanent change
Your fists and guns can't bang
You to a better place
Among the human race.
You will continue to die
By the hands of your brother or
Perhaps of some other who feels threatened
Because your message of being fierce is
Getting through loud and clear.
Love, respect, and value Life
Before the last bang you hear
Claims yours.

Survival Skills

You teach your child survival skills
You hope your child will be strong
So when your child is treated wrong
He/She will only get stronger
But It will take your child longer
To learn the best weapons to use
To protect himself/herself
If you first let your child learn
To get good at using the tools
That losers use.

Lying, stealing, fighting, cheating
There will be no reason
For your child to need them If they prepare for
A life of love, happiness, and success.
Give your child the chance
You may not have had.
Why should his/her childhood
Be as bad yours may have been?
Help your child gain the survival skills
He will need
She will need
In order to succeed
Void of the mess that loser tools leave behind
Messes that will blind your child's view of
A fantastic future
Fueled by a new vision of
What it takes to advance.

Take Time to Listen

Do you take the time to listen to
What's on the mind of your child?
While you are preparing for or chasing after
All the laughter you seek in deep, dark places
Do you know what or who fills the empty spaces
Left in your child's heart?
Do you recall the pain you felt
The times you kept questions to yourself you wanted to ask?
Has time passed too far for you to understand?
You must listen everyday
To what your child has to say.
How else will you know that
He/She is growing
Into the man, into the woman
In whom you can take pride?
Oh yes, you're still young and
You deserve to have fun while you still can,
But remember also, that while you still can
You need to hold the precious little hand of your child and
Instill greatness into his/her heart.
What you place there will grow beyond the child's hand size.
When matured, it will make your child appear foolish or wise.
After a decade of teen-aged rejections
You will reap the benefits of all the corrections
You were able to make because you took the time to listen to
The thoughts on your child's mind
Before it was too late.

Home

Why were you so unkind
When all I was trying to do
Was learn who I was meant to be?
All I can recall now is the hurt I felt
When your words left me
Discouraged and alone.
You made fun of the things I tried to do
To present gifts of pride to you so
I gave up and tucked away my treasures forever.
Now we will never know the value they possessed.

Creating a home is a process.
Home should be a safe haven
Where all who live within are waiting
To exchange love and joy in an atmosphere of peace.
Here, the enemy should not reach you where you rest.
In my childhood home I found less peace than I found out in the streets
Because I heard no words to encourage me to be my best.
I survived.
I passed life's tests and
Today, I feel so blessed and
I've created the home
That should have been created for me.

From Nobody to Somebody

Since so many people repeatedly
Treated me as if I were nobody
I decided that it must be true.
Who was I to disagree with
The same opinion so many others
Had agreed upon about me?
Since who I was had so little value
Then what I did should not have mattered
But it did.
Soon all they wanted was to be rid of me.

I eventually discovered I had a choice and that
I could listen to the Voice encouraging me
From the inside out.
Self-doubt weakened and a beacon of hope
Opened my cloudy world to a bigger, brighter one
Where I am somebody now.

A Good or Bad Man

I never had a dad to love me
To teach me how to tell a good man from a bad one.
The same is true of most of my friends.
Many of the men we know
Show us much more than we
Should be allowed to see.
I have never known how it feels
To give my dad a hug
To thank him for a gift
To express my love in some way
To say something to him that
I would later regret.
I will never get to see him
Look at me with pride.
I never had a dad about whom
I could decide
Whether he, himself, was a good man or
A bad one.

A Child's Secret

To whom do I speak
About the secrets I must keep
About matters happening in my home?
I have gone as far as I can go
And I want someone else to know how
These secrets make me feel.
Until I find someone to trust
I know that I must not
Breathe a word
About the things I've seen and heard
My mother say and do.

She would surely be under arrest and
Would probably love me less
Than she seems to love me now.
How can she let these wrong things be and
Not know how they affect me?
I feel so hurt and confused
Because I cannot get used to all the wrong
I hear and see being all right with me too.
So to whom can I speak and
Who will help me keep
My secrets?

A Blue Sun in a Yellow Sky

I thought that I
Was the only one
Who'd seen a blue sun
In a yellow sky
But I was not.

I was not the first
To labor under the curse
Of being an imperfect son
To the perfect image of a father

For I had not bothered
To question the image
I had created of him.
But once the stories were done
I felt like I'd seen a blue sun
In a yellow sky.

And I wondered why
His tarnished image
Made me laugh
Rather than cry
For all the sons
Who know the pain
Of seeing a blue sun
In a yellow sky.

I Would Have Loved My Daddy

I believe I would have loved my daddy
Had he come around every once in a while.
When I was a child, I only knew him by name.
It was plain to see that
He had no interest in me especially in
Shaping the person I was to be.
He offered me no hand to hold
No protection from the cold I faced
Against my skin neither my heart within.
I have no stories to share about
The time I gave Daddy a scare or about
The time when I had been afraid and
Daddy made me feel safe.
He was not there to encourage my success
Push me past my failures and
Correct the messes
I made before I got things right.
My daddy never put me to bed at night.
He never said one word to me that I can recall.
"There's your daddy," others would point and say or
"I saw your daddy the other day," or
"The older you get, the more like him you look," or
"You took this or that after your daddy."
I would know that for myself and
I would have loved my daddy
Had he taught me these things himself.

The Great Pumping Heart

Back and forth and back again
Circulating information
Among those whose lives
Are stained by sin,
Among the saints,
As well as the saints that ain't,
Like a great heart
Pumping life for the flesh to live,
Likewise the church gives
The black community life.

The Great Pumping Heart
Is the place for any
Community leader to start
If he is to reach the masses.
The lawyer and the man
Who needs a lawyer
Can only be found
On common ground
In the church.

The Great Pumping Heart
Circulates information not only about
Salvation for the soul, but also about
Salvation that leads to self-preservation
In a world from which
Black people must demand their rights.

And so
The Great Pumping Heart
Struggles to pump life and
Hope to parts
Of its community
Overweight with the insanity
Of violent acts of inhumanity
Born out of frustration
Because salvation for the soul
Was not enough to pump.

But the church must ever remember
That a little leaven
Leavens the whole lump
And that Christ died
For the Great Pumping Heart
To pump eternal life.

Still Here

We are still here.
Wipe away your tears and
Let's get to work
Creating something worth
Bleeding, suffering, and dying for.
Pour your heart into
The labor of your hands.
Demand that others
Who work with you
Do the same.

All who understand survival know that
This is not a game.
Our arrival forces us to pick and choose
What we can keep and what we
Can and can't afford to lose.
Create the man we want our boys
To grow and be
Prepare the women and they'll see
That it is so.
They know how to nurture boys and girls
Who can meet the challenges of the world dead on
Just like mothers have done in centuries past.

Cast aside the things that make you appear weak.
We are here still and
Our mothers will have strong, desirable fruit
Among the fruit of other races
Until mankind's last day.

Maternal Grandparents, Nugent and Roberta Vonner

"Black love is Black wealth."

————— ✦✦✦✦✦ —————

—Nikki Giovanni

My childhood home at 728 Lenox was a safe haven. At home, we nurtured our minds and bodies with food, rest, and recreation. We groomed ourselves and made ourselves presentable to others. We settled our differences, managed our emotions, thought our thoughts, dreamt our dreams, and planned our paths forward. We sang, we danced, and we worshipped our God all in our home.

As we grew older, we argued less, and we laughed more. How we laughed! The Bible says in Proverbs 17:22 that laughter is like medicine for the soul. Medical science has proven that laughter improves your health. (Bruce should have lived to be one hundred.) We filled 728 Lenox with laughter from deep within our bellies.

I had an older childhood friend who lived across the street from us. When she became an independent working adult, she moved into the home next door to her parents. She and I would sit on her porch and visit. We could hear laughter coming from my house. She once asked me, "What do y'all be laughing about?" She told me that she would sit on her porch listening to us laugh and ponder answers to her question.

We didn't need much of a reason to burst into laughter. Life was good, and we were grateful. We understood the power of love. We loved each other and being together was so euphoric we could only express it best through our laughter.

When we gathered as adults into each other's homes, we extended the joy we experienced within 728 Lenox and permeated the new environments with familiar love and laughter. Our family home at 728 Lenox was the ancestral home of Judy, Bruce, Rita, Nita, Cheryl, and

229

me. Though we had our own homes, 728 Lenox was everything meaningful found in a loving home twice over. It was The Haliburton Home Squared.

Home Squared

Home Squared is just a myth
Until you get
A home of your own.
Home is where you
Eat, sleep, and make love
Where you plan and dream and
Hope for a better future.

Home is where you go
To retreat and to refresh yourself
From those you know
Will be tomorrow
As they've always been
Lurking, waiting, and hating on you
Ready to pounce.
And once you defend all you love and own
You return home and
Do it all, all over again.

It is there, in your home
In your place of refuge
Like Dorothy
Clicking her heels
To return to a real world
It is there that you recall
The place you call Home Squared.

The smell of something wonderful
Cooking on the stove
The sound of laughter
With the power to rattle the fragile windows
That struggle to keep out the cold in winter.
The sight of all the hands that were blessed
For preparing the tasty meal being delayed
By a lengthy prayer of thanksgiving.
Blessed are they
Who know the way
To a place they can say is for them
Home Squared.

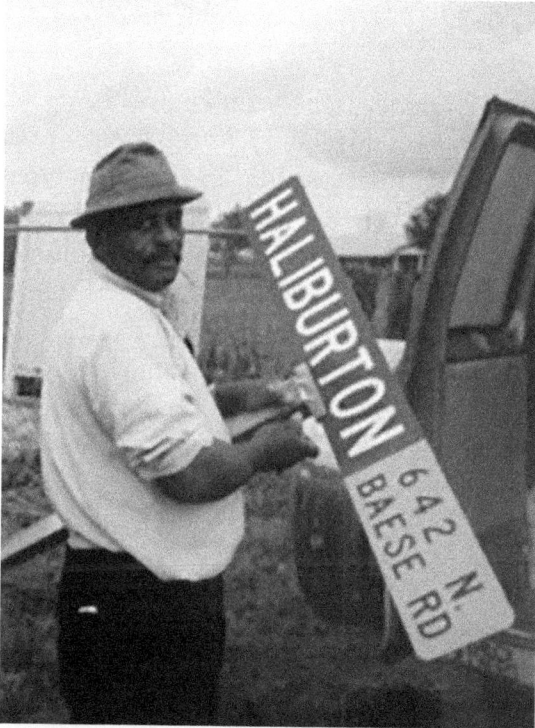

Daddy marks his Home Squared with a street sign.

About the Author

＋＋◆◆◆＋＋

For Waco native Francene Haliburton Francis, being an educator is more than a career. It's a mission! Her story is one of transition, diligence, vision, and spiritual strength. In her thirty-three years as an educator in Waco ISD, she has shared lessons about life, as well as academic lessons with thousands of students and hundreds of colleagues and community stakeholders. She was blessed with parents who loved God and understood how important it was to provide their children with an opportunity to encounter the God of the universe for themselves. She became strong enough and equipped well enough to survive in a world that was not nearly as warm, kind, and caring as the world in which she grew up with her family on Lenox Avenue in Waco, Texas. She is blessed and Living in the Sonshine in Waco, Texas, with her husband, Monty.

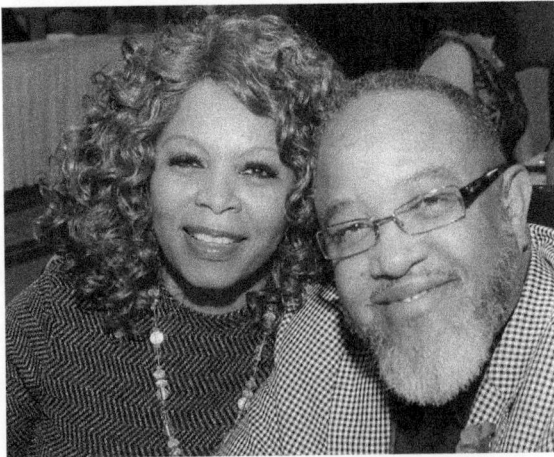

Francene and her husband, Monty

CPSIA information can be obtained
at www.ICGtesting.com
Printed in the USA
FFHW02n1613100918
48271498-52070FF

9 781642 587708